Writing Through Ancient History

Level 1
"Manuscript Models"

A Charlotte Mason Writing Program
"Gentle and Complete"

Ancient History

Historical Narratives, Fables from Aesop, Poetry, and Cultural Tales

BOOKS PUBLISHED BY BROOKDALE HOUSE:

The Writing Through Ancient History books
Writing Through Ancient History Level 1 Cursive Models
Writing Through Ancient History Level 1 Manuscript Models
Writing Through Ancient History Level 2 Cursive Models
Writing Through Ancient History Level 2 Manuscript Models

The Writing Through Medieval History books
Writing Through Medieval History Level 1 Cursive Models
Writing Through Medieval History Level 1 Manuscript Models
Writing Through Medieval History Level 2 Cursive Models
Writing Through Medieval History Level 2 Manuscript Models

The Writing Through Early Modern History Books
Writing Through Early Modern History Level 1 Cursive Models
Writing Through Early Modern History Level 1 Manuscript Models
Writing Through Early Modern History Level 2 Cursive Models
Writing Through Early Modern History Level 2 Manuscript Models

The Writing Through Modern History Books
Writing Through Modern History Level 1 Cursive Models
Writing Through Modern History Level 1 Manuscript Models
Writing Through Modern History Level 2 Cursive Models
Writing Through Modern History Level 2 Manuscript Models

The Fun Spanish Level 1

Sheldon's Primary Language Lessons
(Introductory grammar workbook for elementary students)

The Westminster Shorter Catechism Copybook
(Available in the following font styles: traditional, modern, italic, and vertical, both print and cursive)

The Geography Drawing Series
Drawing Around the World: Europe
Drawing Around the World: USA

Easy Narrative Writing

ISBN: 978-1-64281-034-9

© Copyright 2015. Kimberly Garcia. Published by Brookdale House. Brookdale House grants permission to photocopy pages for use within a single family. All other rights reserved. For permission to make copies, written or otherwise, except for the use within one immediate family, please contact the author at www.brookdalehouse.com or Kimberly@brookdalehouse.com .

Table of Contents

Introduction	v
Definitions—Narration, Copywork, Studied Dictation	vii
Scheduling Information	x

Chapter I — Historical Narratives

The Goddess of the Silkworm, China	c. 2640 BC	I-3
The Mystery of the Lost Brother, Biblical Joseph	c. 1650 BC – c. 1540 BC	I-8
David and Goliath	c. 1037 BC – c. 967 BC	I-16
Saved by a Dolphin, Greek Musician	c. 7th Century BC	I-22
The General and the Fox, Greek general	c. 685 BC	I-28
"BECOS! BECOS! BECOS!" Egyptian Psammeticus	664 BC – 610 BC	I-33
A Clever Slave, Aesop	620 BC - 560 BC	I-39
The Young Cupbearer, Cyrus the Great	c. 590 BC— c. 529 BC	I-44
The Lover of Men, Gautama	c. 563 BC to c. 483 BC	I-50
The Boy and the Robbers, Persia	559 BC-529 BC	I-56
Horatius at the Bridge	c. 6th Century BC	I-61
The Story of Ruth and Naomi	c. 500 BC	I-67
A Story of Old Rome, Coriolanus	c. 5th Century BC	I-72
The Brave Three Hundred, Greek Persian War	c. 480 BC	I-78
Socrates and His House	c. 469 BC– 399 BC	I-83
Two Great Painters	c. born 464 BC	I-87
The Story of Cincinnatus, ruled Rome	457 BC	I-91
Damon and Pythias, friendship	c. 432 BC – c. 367BC	I-97
The Sword of Damocles, Dionysius	c. 4th century BC	I-102
A Laconic Answer, Spartans of Laconia	382 BC – 336 BC	I-107
A Lesson in Justice, Alexander the Great	356 BC –323 BC	I-111
The Story of Regulus	died c. 250 BC	I-117
Julius Caesar	100 BC - 44 BC	I-122
The Visit of the Wise Men	c. 4 BC	I-127
Androclus and the Lion	? 1st century CE *	I-131

Chapter II** — Aesop's Fables

The Bear and the Bees	II-3
The Dog, the Cock, and the Fox	II-7
The Farmer and His Sons	II-11
The Lark and her Young Ones	II-15
Mercury and the Woodman	II-19
The Milkmaid and her Pail	II-24
The Miser	II-28
The Monkey and the Dolphin	II-32
The North Wind and the Sun	II-36
The Shepherd Boy and the Wolf	II-40
The Tortoise and the Ducks	II-44
Two Travelers and a Bear	II-48
The Vain Jackdaw and His Borrowed Feathers	II-52
The Wolf and the Kid	II-56
The Wolf and the Lean Dog	II-60

*Note: The ? indicates that the event may or may not have happened.
**Note: Fables from Aesop

Chapter III — Poetry from/about Ancient History

Age, by Anacreon	c. 570 BC – 480 BC	III-3
The Boaster, Aesop	620 BC - 560 BC	III-6
The Crow and the Pitcher	620 BC - 560 BC	III-9
The Destruction of Sennacherib	705-681 BC	III-12
Horatius (excerpt)	c. 6th Century BC	III-15
Moderation, by Horace	65 BC-8 BC	III-19
The Mouse and the Lion, Aesop	620 BC - 560 BC	III-22
The People Who Are Really Happy, Jesus Christ	c. 4 BC to 33 AD	III-25
Psalms 23 and 121, by King David	c.1037 - 967 BCE	III-28
The Two Paths, Proverbs	c. 1000 BCE - 931 BCE	III-31
The Vision of Belshazzar, Lord Byron	died 539 BC	III-34

Chapter IV⁺ — Cultural Tales

The Bag of Winds	Greek myth	IV-3
Diana and Apollo	Roman myth	IV-9
The Dog and the Dog Dealer	Tale of India	IV-13
The Golden Touch	Greek Myth	IV-17
Great and Little Bear	Greek myth	IV-23
Sennin the Hermit	Tale of Japan	IV-27
The Tricky Wolf and the Rats	Jataka Tale	IV-32

Appendix

Narration Questions	2
Grammar Guide	3
Models from Chapter I historical narratives	8
Models from Chapter II fables from Aesop	13
Models from Chapter III poetry from or about ancient history	15
Models from Chapter IV folktales of various cultures	18

+Note: The publication dates for Chapter IV are not included. These are very old tales with many variations published at various times.

Introduction

Writing Through Ancient History Layout

Writing Through Ancient History is a writing program that teaches grammar, spelling, penmanship, and history—all at once. This volume covers **ancient history, from creation myths to 400 AD,** for the beginning writer.

Writing Through Ancient History teaches writing the Charlotte Mason way for grades first through third. It is divided into four chapters: short stories, fables from Aesop, poetry, and cultural tales. For Chapter I, short stories that give insight into people, places, and events during **ancient times** have been selected. Chapter II contains fables from Aesop. Chapter III contains poetry from and about ancient times. Chapter IV contains folk tales from various cultures.

In all four chapters, the reading selection is followed by two passages, which serve as writing models for the student. The first model has lines immediately below each word and the second model has lines further down the paper. There are more than 55 selections included in ***Writing Through Ancient History***.

To coordinate ***Writing Through Ancient History*** with your history topics, refer to the Table of Contents, which also serves as a timeline. Use the timeline provided to determine which selection would be the best fit for that week's history lesson. ***Writing Through Ancient History*** can be used with any history program.

All of the works included were taken from the public domain; many have been edited for **Writing Through Ancient History**.

Note: Although titles of books and ships would normally be italicized in texts, they are underlined to teach children that these names are underlined in handwritten works.

All of the principles in ***Writing Through Ancient History*** are based on the work of Ms. Charlotte Mason. She advocated that children of the grammar or elementary stage practice narration, copywork, and dictation as their primary method of learning to write. But because Ms. Mason's methods have been interpreted differently over the years, I have included an attachment in the Appendix that offers advice on variations of implementing *Writing Through Ancient History*. So to begin using *Writing Through Ancient History* as your child's writing program, please read all of the introduction, pages v–ix before your student begins.

Additional Information

Reading Levels
Chapters I and II contain chapters taken from living books that are historically relevant to ancient times. These selections may be above the reading ability of some first and second graders. Chapter III contains poetry that will be above the reading level of many first, second, and third graders. If necessary, read the poetry selections to your student. If you would like to stretch your student, ask him to read the selections back to you. These reading selections offer great opportunity to cover new vocabulary as well as new ideas.

Appendix "Models Only"
The Appendix lists all of the models by chapter. The first model is in normal typeface while the second model is italicized. Only the first model follows the reading selections. The second models were added to give the students a different model for dictation. For the sake of organization, the Appendix contains a copy of the models to assist the instructor with copywork and studied dictation.

Getting Started
On the following page, I have covered each area of the program: Narration, Copywork, and Dictation. I have also provided a guide suggesting how to incorporate grammar into the program. Please read these in their entirety.

Correcting Work
Correcting writing, whether written summations, copywork, or dictation, is always difficult. Ms. Mason advised teachers and parents to correct the student's writings occasionally. This makes perfect sense when realizing that Ms. Mason's methods did not require the need for extensive corrections. She consistently emphasized that work be done correctly the first time. She believed that a student should not be allowed to visually dwell on incorrect work. When a child made a mistake during dictation, Ms. Mason had stamps or pieces of paper available to cover the mistakes so that the mistakes were not reinforced visually.

When a child made a mistake during narrations, she withheld correcting him. I believe that she used the time after the oral narration was finished to discuss the material that had been narrated.

When corrections are needed, it is good to practice the principle of praise before correcting children. Find out what is right with what they've done. Be impressed. Focus on their effort. Build them up. Ephesians 5:29 of the King James Bible says—

Let no corrupt communication
proceed out of your mouth, but
that which is good to the use of edifying,
that it may minister grace
unto the hearers.

The hearers are our students—our children. And the words we say will either minister grace or condemnation. We must encourage them and free them from the fear of our frustrations and negative feedback as we correct them.

Definitions

Personal Narrations – the act of retelling

Ms. Mason believed narrations should be done immediately after the story was read to the student or by the student. Narrations are very simple, yet very effective in teaching writing. Narrating helps children to internalize the content of the reading material they have been exposed to and allows them to make it their own. In order to narrate, students must listen carefully, dissect the information, and then express that same information in their own words. It is a powerful tool, but very simple to put into practice.

Oral narrations **Read all or part of the story only once before requiring the student to narrate! It will require him to pay attention.** Simply ask your student to tell you what he has just heard or read.

If your student has trouble with this process, show him how to narrate by demonstrating the process for him. **Read a selection yourself and then narrate it to him. Ask him to imitate you.** If he continues to draw a blank, use the list of questions below to prompt him.

Besides all of the previously mentioned benefits, oral narrations teach students to digest information, dissect it, and reorganize it into their own words while thinking on their feet. This practice helps students to develop the art of public speaking. This formal process will force them to express their ideas without a written plan. It strengthens the mind. And over time, their speech will become fluent and natural. (I sometimes have my children stand as they narrate. It makes the process more formal.)

If your student has difficulty with narrations, ask some or all of the following questions:

1. Who was the main character?
2. What was the character like?
3. Where was the character?
4. What time was it in the story?
5. Who else was in the story?
6. Does the main character have an enemy?
   (The enemy may be another character, himself, or nature.)
7. Did the main character have a problem? If not, what did the character want?
8. What does the main character do? What does he say? If there are others, what do they do?
9. Why does the character do what he does?
10. What happens to the character as he tries to solve his problem?
11. Is there a moral to the story? If so, what was it?
12. What happens at the end of the story? Or how does the main character finally solve his problem?

Written Summations

Most first and second graders will not be ready to write their own summations. Until they are, students dictate and parents write. Written Summations are different from oral narrations. The oral narrations allow the students to demonstrate all that they have learned from the reading selection. Summaries, however, focus on the most important aspects of the selection—the beginning, the middle, and the end as well as the who, what, when, where, why, and how.

Around the age of 10, Ms. Mason required students to write down their narrations, for themselves. Many students can do this earlier. Written summations will allow your student to develop this skill. If your student is able, have him write as much as he can, as perfectly as he can, even around the age of 8.

At the end of each oral narration, ask your child to summarize the reading selection by identifying the beginning, the middle, and the end. He should be able to do this in about three to six sentences. Younger students will sometimes begin each sentence with "First,..." or "At the beginning,..." This is okay. But once the student masters the summation, ask him to summarize without these types of words. Tell him to begin with the subject or the time.

>Ex: When Louisa May Alcott was a young girl, she was very happy because she spent her time playing with her sisters and writing in her diary.

The benefits of written summations are manifold. They will help your student to think linearly from the beginning of the reading selection to the end. They also provide the right amount of content for the beginning writer. When you feel that your student is ready, help his to write the first sentence of his summation; **allow him to dictate the remaining sentences to you.**

Additionally, the act of summarizing teaches students to identify the main thread or central idea of a passage. Even though your child begins to write his written summations, have him continue his oral narrations without limit. These will help him to internalize and learn the historical content of the stories in *Writing Through Ancient History* as well develop his public speaking skills.

Copywork and Grammar—copying a passage exactly as written

As your child copies the model before him, stay near so that you are able to correct any problems immediately. Ms. Mason was a strong advocate in learning a skill correctly the first time.

Before your child begins, discuss the model with him. Point out the grammatical elements that he is learning. Have your child copy the model. If you are studying grammar via the models, have him identify a part of speech in the model and circle it with a colored pencil. See page 3 of the Appendix for a grammar guide. (Spend as long as necessary on each part of speech. This means that some first graders may only cover nouns, verbs, and pronouns during one school year. This is definitely okay!) When using the grammar guide, continue to review by including all previously learned work in the current lesson. Once nouns are learned, the student is to identify both nouns and verbs. Thereafter—nouns, verbs, and pronouns.

Ms. Mason recommended the formal study of grammar at about 4th or 5th grade. If you opt to add a formal program for your beginning writer, that would be fine. If you do so, feel free to omit the grammar study in this program.

The grammar guide contains more grammar than is necessary for first and second graders. At this level, students only focus on learning the parts of speech and the punctuation necessary to correctly write the four types of sentences.

Studied Dictation—the act of writing from an oral reading
(Many students will not be ready for dictation at this level. If you child masters copywork, feel free to introduce dictation.)

Once again, Ms. Mason's ideas are simple, yet effective. The goal in dictation is to teach your child to write correctly, and from memory, the sentences or clauses he has just heard. Ms. Mason let the child study the dictation model for a few minutes. She wrote down any unknown words on a board that were more difficult for him. She then erased the board and read each passage only once. From this one reading, the child wrote; however, if the child made a mistake, Ms. Mason covered the mistake instantly so that the student was not allowed to visualize and internalize it.

If you would like to introduce your second or third grader to dictation, feel free to reduce the model to an appropriate length for your student. For the child who has never done dictation, this may be a sentence of only a few words. Read the passage as many times as necessary. Work down to one reading per sentence. This is an advanced skill and may require time to achieve. Be patient, but consistent. (If needed, allow your student to repeat the model back to you before he writes. Some students may need this reinforcement; others may not.)

After you write the dictation model on the whiteboard, discuss it, in depth, with your student. An example of the process follows.

MODEL

The bolded paragraphs below are the model for this exercise.

"Did Mary spill the ink on the carpet?" asked Tom.
"No," answered Mary. "Did you, Will?"
"I did not, Mary, but I know who did," said Will.
"Who was it, Will?"
Will did not answer in words. He pointed a finger at Fido, and guilty little Fido crept under the sofa.

For the student that is new to dictation, determine the size of the model. In the dialogue above, the bolded words represent the sentences that are to be discussed for studied dictation.

Because the student is new to dictation, do not expect him to understand the grammar if he has not been taught it before. So first, determine which grammatical elements you will be teaching. For this example, we are focusing on proper and common nouns, as well as questions and statements.

QUESTIONS TO ASK:

1. What are the names of the people in this story? How does each name begin?
2. Do you remember what a noun is? A noun is the word that names a person, place, thing, or idea. Can you find any nouns in the first paragraph?
3. Do you see that some nouns are not capitalized and some are?
4. Common nouns are not capitalized. Common nouns name any item of a group—like any boy, girl, or building. However, proper nouns name specific boys, girls, or buildings—Jimmy Brown, Mary Black, or Tom Swift.
5. Do you remember what a question is? Can you find a question mark in the first sentence?
6. Can you make up some questions of your own?
   Sentences that end in question marks are called questions or interrogative sentences.
7. Sentences that end in periods are called declarative sentences or statements. Can you find a period in the first sentence or the second?

If there are any questions that your student cannot answer, tell him the answers. Discuss the grammar with him, and work with him until he can narrate why the model is punctuated the way it is.

Do the same with spelling. Identify the words that your student doesn't know and discuss why those words are spelled the way they are.

To see an example of studied dictation, visit the youtube video at the link below:
https://www.youtube.com/watch?v=xoTACGomwsw

or search "Studied Dictation Demonstration" on youtube.
There I demonstrate this dictation process.

Scheduling Information

Listed below is a recommendation for the use of *Writing Through Ancient History*; however, this is **only a recommendation** and should be adjusted for your student's individual needs. **Further explanations and alternate methods** are included on the next page. Please feel free to adjust these methods to make writing as painless as possible for your student. Every child is different.

One Suggested Schedule:

Day 1 — **Reading, Oral Narration, and Written Summation**
From the Table of Contents, choose a story.
Either you or your student should read the story selection once.
First, have the student orally narrate to you.
If he has difficulty, demonstrate how to narrate and then ask him to imitate you.
If he still cannot narrate the story, use the narration questions listed in the Appendix.
(Optional: ask your student to summarize the story in about three sentences to six sentences. If he is able, have him write one or more sentences from his summation.)
Write for him, if needed.
(For more on narrations, see page vii.)

Day 2 — **Copywork and Grammar** Complete Model Practice 1 from Day 1's reading selection. Discuss/explain the grammar and punctuation in the model.
Do a color-coded grammar study.
(For more on copywork and grammar, see page viii.)
(See page 3 and 4 of the Appendix for the grammar guide)

Day 3 — **Copywork and Grammar** Complete Model Practice 2, also from Day 1's reading selection. Discuss/explain the grammar and punctuation in the model.
Do a color-coded grammar study.
(See page 3 and 4 of the Appendix for the grammar guide)

Day 4 — **Reading, Oral narration, and Copywork**
From the Table of Contents, choose a story or poem.
He may read the poem himself. If so, teach him to read with expression.
Have your student orally narrate what he has learned. Use Model Practice 1 for copywork. Discuss/explain the grammar and punctuation in the model.
Do a color-coded grammar study.
(See page 3 and 4 of the Appendix for the grammar guide)

Day 5 — **Copywork and Grammar** Complete Model Practice 2, also from Day 4's reading selection. Discuss/explain the grammar and punctuation in the model.
Do a color-coded grammar study.
(See page 3 and 4 of the Appendix for the grammar guide)

If the models are too long
If the models are too long for your student, reduce them. Beginning writers should not be forced to do more than they are able.

If your child is ready for dictation
Use either the first or second model as dictation. The Appendix contains a list of all models used in *Writing Through Ancient History*. Remove and use to dictate to your student.

Optional Schedules

Charlotte Mason's Methods

Ms. Mason used narration, copywork, and dictation simultaneously throughout a young child's education. Narrations were done immediately after they had listened to or read the selection. Copywork was done from well-written sentences. And while many don't believe copywork to be valuable once a student learns to write from dictation, Ms. Mason believed that copywork was extremely valuable for many years alongside dictation. Dictation was a separate part of the process, mostly for the purpose of teaching spelling.

Ms. Mason allowed students to look at the dictation passages and study them before the student began writing. This process was helpful because it allowed the student to visualize how the passage should look. It taught him to study with intent and to focus on each individual word. After the passage was read once, the student wrote the passage from memory. This method improved a child's spelling and his grasp of correct punctuation, as well.

But not everyone who follows Ms. Mason's methods follows each area of narration, copywork and dictation in the same way. Below are some ways to incorporate some or all of these ideas into your child's learning adventure.

Different Copywork Passages Daily

If followed, the schedule on the previous page will provide your student with four separate copywork passages per week.

Copywork as Dictation

If you would like to introduce your child to dictation by using the same model, you may use the first model provided as copywork and dictation. Have your student copy the passage on day 2 and write it from dictation on day 3. He should write the dictation work in the model practice 3 area.

Copywork and Dictation

If you would like to use the second model for dictation rather than copywork, cover the passage in the text and dictate the model to your student. You may use the student's model, which is provided in the student's book, for studied dictation. With studied dictation, the student studies the model for unknown words and works on memorizing them. When he is ready, cover the model with a slip of sticky paper and dictate while he writes. The Appendix contains a list of all models for the instructor's use.

More on Studied Dictation

Once again, Ms. Mason's ideas are simple, yet effective. The goal in dictation is to teach your child to write correctly and from memory the sentences or clauses he has just heard. Ms. Mason let the child study the dictation for a few minutes. She wrote on a board any unknown words that were more difficult for him. She then erased the board and read each passage only once. From this one reading, the child wrote; however, if the child made a mistake, she covered the mistake instantly so that the student was not allowed to visualize and internalize the mistake.

For the child who has never done dictation, start by reading as many times as necessary so that your child memorizes the sentences. ***Work down to one reading per model.*** This is an advanced skill and may require time to achieve. Be patient, but consistent. (If needed, allow your student to repeat the model back to you before he writes. Some students may need this reinforcement; others may not.)

Reminders and Helps

- Use *Writing Through Ancient History* in the best way possible to serve your student's needs. Adapt any area, as necessary.
- Help students with spelling, as necessary. Set your student up for success.
- In the case of dialogue, remind your student that each time a different character is speaking, a new paragraph is started via indentions. When they first encounter this, show them an example before requiring them to do this.
- If the size of the selection is too large, **simply reduce it and require less.**
- Set your student up for success. He shouldn't be expected to know what he has not yet been taught.
- To sum up Charlotte Mason's methods:

Quality over quantity.
Accuracy over speed.
Ideas over drill.
Perfection over mediocrity.

Bonus Materials

To learn of new publications and free educational resources, sign up for our newsletter at

www.brookdalehouse.com

or

scan:

CHAPTER I

Historical Narratives from Ancient Times

(Models taken from the beginning of a paragraph in the original selection are indented.)

The Goddess of the Silkworm
c. 2640 BC
from <u>A Child's World Reader</u>
by Hetty Browne, Sarah Withers, and W K. Tate

Hoangti was the emperor of China. He had a beautiful wife whose name was Si-ling. The emperor and his wife loved their people and always thought of their happiness.

In those days, the Chinese people wore clothes made of skins. By and by animals grew scarce, and the people did not know what they should wear. The emperor and empress tried in vain to find some other way of clothing them.

One morning Hoangti and his wife were in the beautiful palace garden. They walked up and down, up and down, talking of their people.

Suddenly the emperor said, "Look at those worms on the mulberry trees, Si-ling. They seem to be spinning."

Si-ling looked, and sure enough, the worms were spinning. A long thread was coming from the mouth of each, and each little worm was winding this thread around its body.

Si-ling and the emperor stood still and watched the worms. "How wonderful!" said Si-ling.

The next morning Hoangti and the empress walked under the trees again. They found some worms still winding thread. Others had already spun their cocoons and were fast asleep. In a few days, all of the worms had spun cocoons.

"This is indeed a wonderful, wonderful thing!" said Si-ling. "Why, each worm has a thread on its body long enough to make a house for itself!"

Si-ling thought of this day after day. One morning as she and the emperor walked under the trees, she said, "I believe I could find a way to weave those long threads into cloth."

"But how could you unwind the threads?" asked the emperor.

"I'll find a way," Si-ling said. And she did, but she had to try many, many times.

She put the cocoons in a hot place, and the little sleepers soon died. Then the cocoons were thrown into boiling water to make the threads soft. After that, the long threads could be easily unwound.

Now Si-ling had to think of something else; she had to find a way to weave the threads into cloth. After many trials, she made a loom—the first that was ever made. She taught others to weave, and soon hundreds of people were making cloth from the threads of the silkworm.

The people ever afterward called Si-ling "The Goddess of the Silkworm." And whenever the emperor walked with her in the garden, they liked to watch the silkworms spinning threads for the good of their people.

Written Summation

Model Practice 1 (adapted from the original)

In those days, the Chinese people wore clothes made of skins. By and by the animals grew scarce.

The next morning Hoangti and the empress walked under the trees again. They found some worms still winding thread.

Model Practice 2

Model Practice 3

The Mystery of the Lost Brother
c. 1650 BC -1540 BC
adapted from the Wonder Book of Bible Stories
by Logan Marshall

The food which Jacob's sons had brought from Egypt did not last long, for Jacob's family was large. Most of his sons were married and had children of their own, so that the children and grandchildren were sixty-six. This did not include the servants who waited on them and the men who cared for Jacob's flocks. So around the tent of Jacob was quite a camp of other tents and an army of people.

When the food that had come from Egypt was nearly eaten up, Jacob said to his sons:

"Go down to Egypt again, and buy some food for us."

And Judah, Jacob's son, the man who years before had urged his brothers to sell Joseph to the Ishmaelites, said to his father: "It is of no use for us to go to Egypt, unless we take Benjamin with us. The man who rules in that land said to us, 'You shall not see my face, unless your youngest brother be with you.'"

And Israel said, "Why did you tell the man that you had a brother? You did me great harm when you told him."

"Why," said Jacob's sons, "we could not help telling him. The man asked us all about our family, 'Is your father yet living? Have you any more brothers?' And we had to tell him, his questions were so close. How should we know that he would say, 'Bring your brother here, for me to see him'?"

And Judah said, "Send Benjamin with me, and I will take care of him. I promise you that I will bring him safely home. If he does not come back, let me bear the blame forever. He must go, or we shall die for want of food; and we might have gone down to Egypt and come home again, if we had not been kept back."

And Jacob said, "If he must go, then he must. But take a present to the man, some of the choicest fruits of the land, some spices, and perfumes, and nuts, and almonds. And take twice as much money, besides the money that was in your sacks. Perhaps that was a mistake, when the money was given back to you. And take your brother Benjamin, and may the Lord God make the mankind to you, so that he will set Simeon free and let you bring Benjamin back. But if it is God's will that I lose my children, I cannot help it."

So ten brothers of Joseph went down a second time to Egypt, Benjamin going in place of Simeon. They came to Joseph's office, the place where he sold grain to the people. There they stood before their brother and bowed as before. Joseph saw that Benjamin was with them. Then he said to his steward, the man who was over his house:

"Make ready a dinner, for all these men shall dine with me today."

When Joseph's brothers found that they were taken into Joseph's house, they were filled with fear. They said to each other:

"We have been taken here on account of the money in our sacks. They will say that we have stolen it, and then they will sell us all for slaves."

But Joseph's steward, the man who was over his house, treated the men kindly; and when they spoke of the money in their sacks, he would not take it again, saying:

"Never fear; your God must have sent you this as a gift. I had your money."

The stewards received the men into Joseph's house and washed their feet, according to the custom of the land. And at noon, Joseph came in to meet them. They brought him the present from their father, and again they bowed before him with their faces on the ground.

And Joseph asked them if they were well and said: "Is your father still living, the old man of whom you spoke? Is he well?"

And they said, "Our father is well and he is living." And again they bowed to Joseph.

And Joseph looked at his younger brother Benjamin, the child of his own mother Rachel, and said:

"Is this your youngest brother, of whom you spoke to me? God be gracious unto you, my son."

And Joseph's heart was so full that he could not keep back the tears. He went in haste to his own room and wept there. Then he washed his face, and came out again, and ordered the table to be set for dinner. They set Joseph's table for himself, as the ruler, and another table for his Egyptian officers, and another for the eleven men from Canaan; for Joseph had brought Simeon out of the prison, and had given him a place with his brothers.

Joseph himself arranged the order of the seats for his brothers. He placed the oldest at the head, and all in order of age down to the youngest. The men wondered at this. They could not see how the ruler of Egypt could know the order of their ages. Then Joseph sent dishes from his table to his brothers. He gave to Benjamin five times as much as to the others.

After dinner, Joseph said to his steward: "Fill the men's sacks with grain, as much as they can carry, and put each man's money in his sack. And put my silver cup in the sack of the youngest, with his money."

The steward did as Joseph had said; and early in the morning the brothers started to go home. A little while afterward, Joseph said to his steward:

"Hasten, follow after the men from Canaan. Say to them, 'Why have you wronged me, after I had treated you kindly? You have stolen my master's silver cup, out of which he drinks.'"

The steward followed the men, and overtook them, and charged them with stealing. And they said to him:

"Why should you talk to us in this manner? We have stolen nothing. Why, we brought back to you the money that we found in our sacks; and is it likely that we would steal from your lord his silver or gold? You may search us, and if you find your master's cup on any of us, let him die, and the rest of us may be sold as slaves."

Then they took down the sacks from the asses and opened them. And in each man's sack was his money, for the second time. And when they came to Benjamin's sack, there was the ruler's silver cup! Then, in the greatest sorrow, they tied up their bags again, and laid them on the asses, and came back to Joseph's palace.

And Joseph said to them:

"What wicked thing is this that you have done? Did you not know that I would surely find out your deeds?"

Then Judah said, "O, my lord, what can we say? God has punished us for our sins; and now we must all be slaves, both we that are older, and the younger in whose sack the cup was found."

"What wicked thing is this that you have done?"

"No," said Joseph. "Only one of you is guilty; the one who has taken away my cup. I will hold him as a slave, and the rest of you can go home to your father.

Joseph wished to see whether his brothers were still selfish and were willing to let Benjamin suffer, if they could escape.

Then Judah, the very man who had urged his brothers to sell Joseph as a slave, came forward and fell at Joseph's feet, and pleaded with him to let Benjamin go. He said:

"I promised to bear the blame, if this boy was not brought home in safety. If he does not go back it will kill my poor old father, who has seen much trouble. Now let my youngest brother go home to his father, and I will stay here as a slave in his place!"

Joseph knew now, what he had longed to know. His brothers were no longer cruel nor selfish, but one of them was willing to suffer, so that his brother might be spared. And Joseph could not any longer keep his secret, for his heart longed after his brothers; and he was ready to weep again, with tears of love and joy. He sent all of his Egyptian servants out of the room, so that he might be alone with his brothers, and then he said:

"Come near to me; I wish to speak with you." And they came near, wondering.

Then Joseph said: "I am Joseph. Is my father really alive?"

How frightened his brothers were, as they heard these words spoken in their own language by the ruler of Egypt. For the first time they knew that this stern man, who had their lives in his hand, was their own brother whom they had wronged! Then Joseph said again:

"I am Joseph, your brother, whom you sold into Egypt. But do not feel troubled because of what you did. For God sent me before you to save your lives. There have been already two years of need and famine, and there are to be five years more, when there shall neither be plowing of the fields nor harvest. It was not you who sent me here, but God; and he sent me to save your lives. God has made me like a father to Pharaoh and ruler over all the land of Egypt. Now I wish you to go home and to bring down to me my father and all his family."

Then Joseph placed his arms around Benjamin's neck, kissed him, and wept upon him. And Benjamin wept on his neck. And Joseph kissed all his brothers, to show them that he had fully forgiven them; and after that his brothers began to lose their fear of Joseph and talked with him more freely.

Afterward Joseph sent his brothers home with good news, and rich gifts, and abundant food. He sent also wagons in which Jacob and his sons' wives and the little ones of their families might ride from Canaan down to Egypt. And Joseph's brothers went home happier than they had been for many years.

Written Summation

Model Practice 1

When Joseph's brothers

found that they were

taken into Joseph's house,

they were filled with fear.

Then Joseph placed his arms around Benjamin's neck, kissed him, and wept upon him. And Benjamin wept on his neck.

Model Practice 2

Model Practice 3

David and Goliath
c.1037 BC – c. 967 BC
adapted from a Beacon Reader
adapted from the Bible by James H. Fassett

Long, long ago there lived in the country of Israel a boy named David. He was a shepherd boy, and all day long, he watched the quiet sheep as they ate sweet grass on the hillside.

Although David was only a boy, he was tall and strong and brave. When he knew he was in the right, he feared nothing. David's quiet life did not last long.

There was a great war between the people of Israel and men called the Philistines. All the strong men in David's town went to join the army of Israel. David could not go, as he had to tend the sheep, but his three older brothers went to the war.

For a long time David's father heard nothing from his three oldest boys. At length he called David to him and said, "Take to your brothers a bag of this corn and these ten loaves of bread. Find out how your brothers are, and bring word to me."

The next morning David rose very early, and taking the bag of corn and the loaves of bread, he went to the camp where his brothers were. The camp of Israel was on the side of a high mountain.

Across the valley from this mountain and on the side of another mountain was the camp of the Philistines. After David had come to the camp and had found his brothers, shouts of anger and fear came from the soldiers.

David looked across the valley to the camp of the Philistines. There he saw a huge soldier dressed in shining armor. This giant soldier carried a great spear and shield.

"Who is that man?" asked David.

"Do you not know? That is Goliath," said the soldiers. "Every day he comes out and dares any man on our side to meet him in battle."

"Do none of our soldiers dare to meet him?" asked David.

The giant from the opposite hillside shouted with a loud voice.

"We have no man so strong as he in our whole army," said the soldiers.

The giant from the opposite hillside shouted with a loud voice and again dared the army of Israel to choose a man to meet him.

David was a brave boy; he was stirred to anger at the sight of this great giant.

"Is not God on the side of our people?" he asked. "I will fight with this man, even though he kill me."

The king of Israel heard of these brave words and sent for David to come before him. When he saw that David was only a boy, he said, "You are not able to go against this Philistine. You are only a boy, while he has fought in many battles."

Then David said to the king, "Once, when I was guarding my father's sheep, I killed a lion and a bear without help from any one but the Lord. He will help me fight this man."

Then the king said, "Go, and the Lord be with you."

The king fitted David with heavy armor and gave to him his own sword, but David said, "I am not used to this heavy armor; it will only hinder me." So he threw it off.

Then David went to a brook near by and chose five smooth stones. Armed with these five stones and his sling, he went bravely out to meet the giant.

When the giant saw that David was only a boy, he was angry and cried out:

"Do you dare fight with me? I will kill you and will give your flesh to the birds and the beasts."

David looked at him without fear and said, "You come against me with a sword and with a spear and with a shield, but I come to you in the name of the Lord. This day will he give you into my hand. I will kill you and take your head from you, and I will give the bodies of the Philistines to the birds and the beasts."

When they came near to each other, David fitted one of the five stones to his sling. He whirled the sling swiftly about his head. The stone flew straight to its mark. It struck the Philistine full in the forehead. The huge giant took one step and, with a groan, fell to the earth.

Then David, standing upon the giant, took his sword and cut off the head of his enemy.

When the Philistines saw that their giant was dead, they were filled with fear. They left their camp and tried to run away, but the army of Israel followed them and won a great victory.

For this brave deed David was made a captain and was held in honor by the king.

Written Summation

Model Practice 1

Although David was only a boy, he was tall and strong and brave. When he knew he was in the right, he feared nothing.

David looked across the valley to the camp of the Philistines. There he saw a huge soldier dressed in shining armor.

Model Practice 2

Model Practice 3

Saved by a Dolphin

c. 7th Century BC
from Fifty Famous People
by James Baldwin

In the city of Corinth there once lived a wonderful musician whose name was Arion. No other person could play on the lyre or sing so sweetly as he; and the songs which he composed were famous in many lands.

The king of Corinth was his friend. The people of Corinth never grew tired of praising his sweet music.

One summer he went over the sea to Italy; for his name was well known there, and many people wished to hear him sing.

He visited several cities, and in each place he was well paid for his music.

At last, having become quite rich, he decided to go home. There was a ship just ready to sail for Corinth, and the captain agreed to take him as a passenger.

The sea was rough. The ship was driven far out of her course. Many days passed before they came in sight of land.

The sailors were rude and unruly. The captain himself had been a robber.

When they heard that Arion had a large sum of money with him they began to make plans to get it.

"The easiest way," said the captain, "is to throw him overboard. Then there will be no one to tell tales."

Arion overheard them plotting.

"You may take everything that I have," he said, "if you will only spare my life."

But they had made up their minds to get rid of him. They feared to spare him lest he should report the matter to the king.

"Your life we will not spare," they said; "but we will give you the choice of two things. You must either jump overboard into the sea or be slain with your own sword. Which shall it be?"

"I shall jump overboard," said Arion, "but I pray that you will first grant me a favor."

"What is it?" asked the captain.

"Allow me to sing to you my latest and best song. I promise that as soon as it is finished I will leap into the sea."

The sailors agreed, for they were anxious to hear the musician whose songs were famous all over the world.

Arion dressed himself in his finest clothing. He took his stand on the forward deck, while the robber sailors stood in a half circle before him, anxious to listen to his song.

He touched his lyre and began to play the accompaniment. Then he sang a wonderful song, so sweet, so lively, so touching, that many of the sailors were moved to tears.

And now they would have spared him; but he was true to his promise. As soon as the song was finished, he threw himself headlong into the sea.

The sailors divided his money among themselves; and the ship sailed on. In a short time they reached Corinth in safety, and the king sent an officer to bring the captain and his men to the palace.

"Are you lately from Italy?" he asked.

"We are," they answered.

"What news can you give me concerning my friend Arion, the sweetest of all musicians?"

"He was well and happy when we left Italy," they answered. "He has a mind to spend the rest of his life in that country."

Hardly had they spoken these words when the door opened and Arion himself stood before them. He was dressed just as they had seen him when he jumped into the sea. They were so astonished that they fell upon their knees before the king and confessed their crime.

Now, how was Arion saved from drowning when he leaped overboard?

Old storytellers say that he alighted on the back of a large fish, called a dolphin, which had been charmed by his music and was swimming near the ship. The dolphin carried him with great speed to the nearest shore. Then, full of joy, the musician hastened to Corinth, not stopping even to change his dress.

He told his wonderful story to the king; but the king would not believe him.

"Wait," said he, "till the ship arrives, and then we shall know the truth." Three hours later, the ship came into port, as you have already learned. Other people think that the dolphin which saved Arion was not a fish, but a ship named the *Dolphin.* They say that Arion, being a good swimmer, kept himself afloat until this ship happened to pass by and rescued him from the waves.

You may believe the story that you like best. The name of Arion is still remembered as that of a most wonderful musician.

Written Summation

Model Practice 1

The sea was rough.

The ship was driven far out of her course. Many days passed before they came in sight of land.

But they had made up their minds to get rid of him. They feared to spare him lest he should report the matter to the king.

Model Practice 2

Model Practice 3

The General and the Fox

c. 685 BC
from Fifty Famous People
by James Baldwin

There was once a famous Greek general whose name was Aristomenes. He was brave and wise; and his countrymen loved him.

Once, however, in a great battle with the Spartans, his army was beaten and he was taken prisoner.

In those days, people had not learned to be kind to their enemies. In war, they were savage and cruel; for war always makes men so.

The Spartans hated Aristomenes. He had given them a great deal of trouble, and they wished to destroy him.

On a mountain near their city, there was a narrow chasm or hole in the rocks. It was very deep, and there was no way to climb out of it.

The Spartans said to one another, "Let us throw this fellow into the rocky chasm. Then we may be sure that he will never trouble us again."

So a party of soldiers led him up into the mountain and placed him on the edge of the yawning hole in the rocks. "See the place to which we send all our enemies," they said. And they threw him in.

No one knows how he escaped being dashed to pieces. Some of the Greeks said that an eagle caught him in her beak and carried him unharmed to the bottom. But that is not likely.

I think that he must have fallen upon some bushes and vines that grew in some parts of the chasm. At any rate, he was not hurt much.

He groped around in the dim light, but could not find any way of escape. The rocky walls surrounded him on every side. There was no place where he could set his foot to climb out.

For three days he lay in his strange prison. He grew weak from hunger and thirst. He expected to die from starvation.

Suddenly he was startled by a noise close by him. Something was moving among the rocks at the bottom of the chasm. He watched quietly, and soon saw a large fox coming towards him.

He lay quite still till the animal was very near. Then he sprang up quickly and seized it by the tail.

The frightened fox scampered away as fast as it could; and Aristomenes followed, clinging to its tail. It ran into a narrow cleft, which he had not seen before, and then through a long, dark passage which was barely large enough for a man's body.

Aristomenes held on. At last he saw a ray of light far ahead of him. It was the sunlight streaming in at the entrance to the passage. But soon the way became too narrow for his body to pass through. What should he do? He let go of the fox, and it ran out. Then with great labor he began to widen the passageway. Here the rocks were smaller, and he soon loosened them enough to allow him to squeeze through. In a short time he was free and in the open air.

Some days after this the Spartans heard strange news: "Aristomenes is again at the head of the Greek army." They could not believe it.

Written Summation

Model Practice 1 (adapted from the original)

On a mountain near their city, there was a narrow chasm or hole in the rocks. It was very deep.

The rocky walls surrounded him on every side. There was no place where he could set his foot to climb out.

Model Practice 2

Model Practice 3

"BECOS! BECOS! BECOS!"
664 BC – 610 BC
from Fifty Famous People
by James Baldwin

Thousands of years ago, the greatest country in the world was Egypt.

It was a beautiful land lying on both sides of the wonderful river Nile. In it were many great cities; and from one end of it to the other there were broad fields of grain and fine pastures for sheep and cattle.

The people of Egypt were very proud; for they believed that they were the first and oldest of all nations.

"It was in our country that the first men and women lived," they said. "All the people of the world were once Egyptians."

A king of Egypt, whose name was Psammeticus, wished to make sure whether this was true or not. How could he find out?

He tried first one plan and then another; but none of them proved anything at all. Then he called his wisest men together and asked them, "Is it really true that the first people in the world were Egyptians?"

They answered, "We cannot tell you, O King; for none of our histories go back so far."

Then Psammeticus tried still another plan.

He sent out among the poor people of the city and found two little babies who had never heard a word spoken. He gave these to a shepherd and ordered him to bring them up among his sheep, far from the homes of men. "You must never speak a word to them," said the king; "and you must not permit any person to speak in their hearing."

The shepherd did as he was bidden. He took the children far away to a green valley where his flocks were feeding. There he cared for them with love and kindness; but no word did he speak in their hearing.

They grew up healthy and strong. They played with the lambs in the field and saw no human being but the shepherd.

Thus two or three years went by. Then, one evening when the shepherd came home from a visit to the city, he was delighted to see the children running out to meet him. They held up their hands, as though asking for something, and cried out, "Becos! Becos! Becos!"

The shepherd led them gently back to the hut and gave them their usual supper of bread and milk. He said nothing to them, but wondered where they had heard the strange word "becos," and what was its meaning.

After that, whenever the children were hungry, they cried out, "Becos! Becos! Becos!" till the shepherd gave them something to eat.

Some time later, the shepherd went to the city and told the king that the children had learned to speak one word, but how or from whom, he did not know.

"What is that word?" asked the king.

"Becos."

Then the king called one of the wisest scholars in Egypt and asked him what the word meant.

"Becos," said the wise man, "is a Phrygian word, and it means *bread*."

"Then what shall we understand by these children being able to speak a Phrygian word which they have never heard from other lips?" asked the king.

"We are to understand that the Phrygian language was the first of all languages," was the answer. "These children are learning it just as the first people who lived on the earth learned it in the beginning."

"Therefore," said the king, "must we conclude that the Phrygians were the first and oldest of all the nations?"

"Certainly," answered the wise man.

And from that time the Egyptians always spoke of the Phrygians as being of an older race than themselves.

This was an odd way of proving something, for, as everyone can readily see, it proved nothing.

Written Summation

Model Practice 1

"It was in our country
that the first men and
women lived," they said.
"All the people of the world
were once Egyptians."

The shepherd did as he was bidden. He took the children far away to a green valley where his flocks were feeding.

Model Practice 2

Model Practice 3

A Clever Slave

620 BC - 560 BC
from <u>Fifty Famous People</u>
by James Baldwin

A long time ago there lived a poor slave whose name was Aesop. He was a small man with a large head and long arms. His face was white, but very homely. His large eyes were bright and snappy.

When Aesop was about twenty years old his master lost a great deal of money and was obliged to sell his slaves. To do this, he had to take them to a large city where there was a slave market.

The city was far away, and the slaves must walk the whole distance. A number of bundles were made up for them to carry. Some of these bundles contained the things they would need on the road; some contained clothing; and some contained goods which the master would sell in the city.

"Choose your bundles, boys," said the master. "There is one for each of you."

Aesop at once chose the largest one. The other slaves laughed and said he was foolish. But he threw it upon his shoulders and seemed well satisfied. The next day, the laugh was the other way. For the bundle which he had chosen had contained the food for the whole party. After all had eaten three meals from it, it was very much lighter. And before the end of the journey Aesop had nothing to carry, while the other slaves were groaning under their heavy loads.

"Aesop is a wise fellow," said his master. "The man who buys him must pay a high price."

A very rich man, whose name was Xanthus, came to the slave market to buy a servant. As the slaves stood before him he asked each one to tell what kind of work he could do. All were eager to be bought by Xanthus because they knew he would be a kind master. So each one boasted of his skill in doing some sort of labor. One was a fine gardener; another could take care of horses; a third was a good cook; a fourth could manage a household.

"And what can you do, Aesop?" asked Xanthus.

"Nothing," he answered.

"Nothing? How is that?"

"Because, since these other slaves do everything, there is nothing left for me to perform," said Aesop.

This answer pleased the rich man so well that he bought Aesop at once, and took him to his home on the island of Samos.

In Samos the little slave soon became known for his wisdom and courage. He often amused his master and his master's friends by telling droll fables about birds and beasts that could talk. They saw that all these fables taught some great truth, and they wondered how Aesop could have thought of them.

Many other stories are told of this wonderful slave. His master was so much pleased with him that he gave him his freedom. Many great men were glad to call him their friend, and even kings asked his advice and were amused by his fables.

Written Summation

Model Practice 1

He was a small man with

a large head and long arms.

His face was white, but very

homely. His large eyes

were bright and snappy.

Aesop at once chose the largest one. The other slaves laughed and said he was foolish.

Model Practice 2

Model Practice 3

The Young Cupbearer

c. 590 BC — c. 529 BC Cyrus the Great
from Fifty Famous People
by James Baldwin

Long, long ago, there lived in Persia a little prince whose name was Cyrus.

He was not petted and spoiled like many other princes. Although his father was a king, Cyrus was brought up like the son of a common man.

He knew how to work with his hands. He ate only the plainest food. He slept on a hard bed. He learned to endure hunger and cold.

When Cyrus was twelve years old he went with his mother to Media to visit his grandfather. His grandfather, whose name was Astyages, was king of Media. And he was very rich and powerful.

Cyrus was so tall and strong and handsome that his grandfather was very proud of him. He wished the lad to stay with him in Media. He therefore gave him many beautiful gifts and everything that could please a prince. One day King Astyages planned to make a great feast for the lad. The tables were to be laden with all kinds of food. There was to be music and dancing; and Cyrus was to invite as many guests as he chose. The hour for the feast came. Everything was ready. The servants were there, dressed in fine uniforms. The musicians and dancers were in their places. But no guests came.

"How is this, my dear boy?" asked the king. "The feast is ready, but no one has come to partake of it."

"That is because I have not invited any one," said Cyrus." In Persia we do not have such feasts. If any one is hungry, he eats some bread and meat, with perhaps a few cresses, and that is the end of it. We never go to all this trouble and expense of making a fine dinner in order that our friends may eat what is not good for them."

King Astyages did not know whether to be pleased or displeased.

"Well," said he, "all these rich foods that were prepared for the feast are yours. What will you do with them?"

"I think I will give them to our friends," said Cyrus.

So he gave one portion to the king's officer who had taught him to ride. Another portion he gave to an old servant who waited upon his grandfather. And the rest he divided among the young women who took care of his mother.

The king's cupbearer, Sarcas, was very much offended because he was not given a share of the feast. The king also wondered why this man, who was his favorite, should be so slighted.

"Why didn't you give something to Sarcas?" he asked.

"Well, truly," said Cyrus, "I do not like him. He is proud and overbearing. He thinks that he makes a fine figure when he waits on you."

"And so he does," said the king. "He is very skillful as a cupbearer."

"That may be so," answered Cyrus, "but if you will let me be your cupbearer tomorrow, I think I can serve you quite as well."

King Astyages smiled. He saw that Cyrus had a will of his own, and this pleased him very much.

"I shall be glad to see what you can do," he said. "Tomorrow, you shall be the king's cupbearer."

You would hardly have known the young prince when the time came for him to appear before his grandfather. He was dressed in the rich uniform of the cupbearer, and he came forward with much dignity and grace.

He carried a white napkin upon his arm, and held the cup of wine very daintily with three of his fingers.

His manners were perfect. Sarcas himself could not have served the king half so well.

"Bravo! Bravo!" cried his mother, her eyes sparkling with pride.

"You have done well" said his grandfather. "But you neglected one important thing. It is the rule and custom of the cupbearer to pour out a little of the wine and taste it before handing the cup to me. This you forgot to do."

"Indeed, grandfather, I did not forget it," answered Cyrus.

"Then why didn't you do it?" asked his mother.

"Because I believed there was poison in the wine."

"Poison, my boy!" cried King Astyages, much alarmed. "Poison! Poison!"

"Yes, grandfather, poison. For the other day, when you sat at dinner with your officers, I noticed that the wine made you act queerly. After the guests had drunk quite a little of it, they began to talk foolishly and sing loudly; and some of them went to sleep. And you, grandfather, were as bad as the rest. You forgot that you were king. You forgot all your good manners. You tried to dance and fell upon the floor. I am afraid to drink anything that makes men act in that way."

"Didn't you ever see your father behave so?" asked the king.

"No, never," said Cyrus. "He does not drink merely to be drinking. He drinks to quench his thirst, and that is all."

When Cyrus became a man, he succeeded his father as king of Persia; he also succeeded his grandfather Astyages as king of Media. He was a very wise and powerful ruler, and he made his country the greatest of any that was then known. In history he is commonly called Cyrus the Great.

Written Summation

Model Practice 1 (adapted from the original)

He knew how to work with his hands. He ate only the plainest food. And he slept on a hard bed.

King Astyages smiled. He saw that Cyrus had a will of his own, and this pleased him very much.

Model Practice 2

Model Practice 3

The Lover of Men

c. 563 BCE to 483 BCE
from Fifty Famous People
by James Baldwin

In the Far East there was once a prince whose name was Gautama. He lived in a splendid palace where there was everything that could give delight. It was the wish of his father and mother that every day of his life should be a day of perfect happiness.

So this prince grew up to be a young man, tall and fair and graceful. He had never gone beyond the beautiful gardens that surrounded his father's palace. He had never seen nor heard of sorrow or sickness or poverty. Everything that was evil or disagreeable had been carefully kept out of his sight. He knew only of those things that give joy and health and peace.

But one day after he had become a man, he said: "Tell me about the great world which, you say, lies outside of these palace walls. It must be a beautiful and happy place; and I wish to know all about it."

"Yes, it is a beautiful place," was the answer. "In it there are numberless trees and flowers and rivers and waterfalls, and other things to make the heart glad."

"Then tomorrow I will go out and see some of those things," he said.

His parents and friends begged him not to go. They told him that there were beautiful things at home—why go away to see other things less beautiful? But when they saw that his mind was set on going, they said no more.

The next morning, Gautama sat in his carriage and rode out from the palace into one of the streets of the city. He looked with wonder at the houses on either side, and at the faces of the children who stood in the doorways as he passed. At first, he did not see anything that disturbed him; for word had gone before him to remove from sight everything that might be displeasing or painful.

Soon the carriage turned into another street--a street less carefully guarded. Here there were no children at the doors. But suddenly, at a narrow place, they met a very old man, hobbling slowly along over the stony way.

"Who is that man?" asked Gautama, "and why is his face so pinched and his hair so white? Why do his legs tremble under him as he walks, leaning upon a stick? He seems weak, and his eyes are dull. Is he some new kind of man?"

"Sir," answered the coachman, "that is an old man. He has lived more than eighty years. All who reach old age must lose their strength and become like him, feeble and gray."

"Alas!" said the prince. "Is this the condition to which I must come?"

"If you live long enough," was the answer.

"What do you mean by that? Do not all persons live eighty years—yes, many times eighty years?"

The coachman made no answer, but drove onward.

They passed out into the open country and saw the cottages of the poor people. By the door of one of these a sick man was lying upon a couch, helpless and pale.

"Why is that man lying there at this time of day?" asked the prince. "His face is white, and he seems very weak. Is he also an old man?"

"Oh, no! He is sick," answered the coachman. "Poor people are often sick."

"What does that mean?" asked the prince. "Why are they sick?"

The coachman explained as well as he was able; and they rode onward.

Soon they saw a company of men toiling by the roadside. Their faces were browned by the sun; their hands were hard and gnarly; their backs were bent by much heavy lifting; their clothing was in tatters.

"Who are those men, and why do their faces look so joyless?" asked the prince. "What are they doing by the roadside?"

"They are poor men, and they are working to improve the king's highway," was the answer.

"Poor men? What does that mean?"

"Most of the people in the world are poor," said the coachman. "Their lives are spent in toiling for the rich. Their joys are few; their sorrows are many."

"And is this the great, beautiful, happy world that I have been told about?" cried the prince. "How weak and foolish I have been to live in idleness and ease while there is so much sadness and trouble around me. Turn the carriage quickly, coachman, and drive home. Henceforth, I will never again seek my own pleasure. I will spend all my life, and give all that I have, to lessen the distress and sorrow with which this world seems filled."

This the prince did. One night he left the beautiful palace which his father had given to him and went out into the world to do good and to help his fellow men. And to this day, millions of people remember and honor the name of Gautama, as that of the great lover of men.

Written Summation

Model Practice 1

He knew only of those things that give joy and health and peace.

They passed out into the open country and saw the cottages of the poor people.

Model Practice 2

Model Practice 3

The Boy and the Robbers
559 BC-529 BC reign of Cyrus the Great
from Fifty Famous People
by James Baldwin

In Persia, when Cyrus the Great was king, boys were taught to tell the truth. This was one of their first lessons at home and at school.

"None but a coward will tell a falsehood," said the father of young Otanes.

"Truth is beautiful. Always love it," said his mother.

When Otanes was twelve years old, his parents wished to send him to a distant city to study in a famous school that was there. It would be a long journey and a dangerous one. So it was arranged that the boy should travel with a small company of merchants who were going to the same place. "Good-by, Otanes! Be always brave and truthful," said his father. "Farewell, my child! Love that which is beautiful. Despise that which is base," said his mother.

The little company began its long journey. Some of the men rode on camels, some on horses. They went but slowly, for the sun was hot and the way was rough.

Suddenly, towards evening, a band of robbers swooped down upon them. The merchants were not fighting men. They could do nothing but give up all their goods and money.

"Well, boy, what have you got?" asked one of the robbers, as he pulled Otanes from his horse.

"Forty pieces of gold" answered the lad.

The robber laughed. He had never heard of a boy with so much money as that.

"That is a good story" he said. "Where do you carry your gold?"

"It is in my hat, underneath the lining," answered Otanes.

"Oh, well! You can't make me believe that," said the robber; and he hurried away to rob one of the rich merchants.

Soon another came up and said, "My boy, do you happen to have any gold about you?"

"Yes! Forty pieces, in my hat," said Otanes.

"You are a brave lad to be joking with robbers" said the man; and he also hurried on to a more promising field.

At length the chief of the band called to Otanes and said, "Young fellow, have you anything worth taking?"

Otanes answered, "I have already told two of your men that I have forty pieces of gold in my hat. But they wouldn't believe me."

"Take off your hat," said the chief.

The boy obeyed. The chief tore out the lining and found the gold hidden beneath it.

"Why did you tell us where to find it?" he asked. "No one would have thought that a child like you had gold about him."

"If I had answered your questions differently, I should have told a lie," said Otanes; "and none but cowards tell lies."

The robber chief was struck by this answer. He thought of the number of times that he himself had been a coward. Then he said, "You are a brave boy, and you may keep your gold. Here it is. Mount your horse, and my own men will ride with you and see that you reach the end of your journey in safety."

Otanes, in time, became one of the famous men of his country. He was the advisor and friend of two of the kings who succeeded Cyrus.

Written Summation

Model Practice 1 (adapted from the original)

Suddenly, towards evening, a band of robbers swooped down upon them. The merchants were not fighting men. They could do nothing.

"If I had answered your questions differently, I should have told a lie," said Otanes; "and none but cowards tell lies."

Model Practice 2

Model Practice 3

Horatius at the Bridge

c. 6th Century BC
from Fifty Famous Stories Retold
by James Baldwin

Once there was a war between the Roman people and the Etruscans who lived in the towns on the other side of the Tiber River. Porsena, the King of the Etruscans, raised a great army, and marched toward Rome. The city had never been in so great danger.

The Romans did not have very many fighting men at that time, and they knew that they were not strong enough to meet the Etruscans in open battle. So they kept themselves inside of their walls, and set guards to watch the roads.

One morning the army of Porsena was seen coming over the hills from the north. There were thousands of horsemen and footmen, and they were marching straight toward the wooden bridge which spanned the river at Rome.

"What shall we do?" said the white-haired Fathers who made the laws for the Roman people. "If they once gain the bridge, we cannot hinder them from crossing; and then what hope will there be for the town?"

Now, among the guards at the bridge, there was a brave man named Horatius. He was on the farther side of the river, and when he saw that the Etruscans were so near, he called out to the Romans who were behind him.

"Hew down the bridge with all the speed that you can!" he cried. "I, with the two men who stand by me, will keep the foe at bay."

Then, with their shields before them, and their long spears in their hands, the three brave men stood in the road, and kept back the horsemen whom Porsena had sent to take the bridge.

On the bridge the Romans hewed away at the beams and posts. Their axes rang, the chips flew fast; and soon it trembled and was ready to fall.

"Come back! Come back, and save your lives!" they cried to Horatius, and the two who were with him.

But just then Porsena's horsemen dashed toward them again.

"Run for your lives!" said Horatius to his friends. "I will keep the road."

They turned and ran back across the bridge. They had hardly reached the other side when there was a crashing of beams and timbers. The bridge toppled over to one side and then fell with a great splash into the water.

When Horatius heard the sound, he knew that the city was safe. With his face still toward Porsena's men, he moved slowly backward till he stood on the river's bank. A dart thrown by one of Porsena's soldiers put out his left eye; but he did not falter. He cast his spear at the fore-most horseman, and then he turned quickly around. He saw the white porch of his own home among the trees on the other side of the stream;

> "And he spake to the noble river
> That rolls by the walls of Rome:
> 'O Tiber! Father Tiber!
> To whom the Romans pray,
> A Roman's life, a Roman's arms,
> Take thou in charge to-day.'"

He leaped into the deep, swift stream. He still had his heavy armor on; and when he sank out of sight, no one thought that he would ever be seen again. But he was a strong man and the best swimmer in Rome. The next minute he rose. He was halfway across the river and safe from the spears and darts which Porsena's soldiers hurled after him.

Soon he reached the farther side, where his friends stood ready to help him. Shout after shout greeted him as he climbed upon the bank. Then Porsena's men shouted also, for they had never seen a man so brave and strong as Horatius. He had kept them out of Rome, but he had done a deed which they could not help but praise.

As for the Romans, they were very grateful to Horatius for having saved their city. They called him Horatius Cocles, which meant the "one-eyed Horatius," because he had lost an eye in defending the bridge; they caused a fine statue of brass to be made in his honor; and they gave him as much land as he could plow around in a day. And for hundreds of years afterwards—

>"With weeping and with laughter,
>Still was the story told,
>How well Horatius kept the bridge
>In the brave days of old."

Written Summation

Model Practice 1

A dart thrown by one of Porsena's soldiers put out his left eye, but he did not falter.

But he was a strong man and the best swimmer in Rome. The next minute he rose.

Model Practice 2

Model Practice 3

The Story of Ruth and Naomi

c. 500 BC
adapted from Good Cheer Stories Every Child Should Know
adapted from the Bible by C. S. Bailey and C. M. Lewis

Now it came to pass, many hundreds of years ago, that there was a good woman named Naomi. Naomi lived in the land of the Moabites. She had once been very rich and happy, but now her husband was dead and her two sons also. She had left only Orpah and Ruth, the wives of her sons. There was a famine in the land. Naomi could find no grain in the fields to beat into flour. She and Orpah and Ruth were lonely and sad and very hungry.

But Naomi heard there was a land where the Lord had visited His people and given them bread. So she went forth from the place where she was, and her two daughters with her, to the land called Judah. It was a long, hard way to go. There were rough roads to travel and steep hills to climb. Their feet grew so weary they could scarcely walk, and at last Naomi said:

"Go, return each to your father's house. The Lord deal kindly with you as you have dealt with me. The Lord grant you that you may find rest."

Then she kissed them. And Orpah kissed her and left her, but Ruth would not leave Naomi. And Naomi said to Ruth:

"Behold, thy sister is gone back unto her own people. Return thou!"

But Ruth clung to Naomi more closely, as she said:

"Entreat me not to leave thee, or to return from following after thee. For whither thou goest, there will I go; and where thou lodgest, there will I lodge. Thy people shall be my people, and thy God my God."

When Naomi saw that Ruth loved her so much, she forgot how tired and hungry she was. And the two journeyed on together until they came to Bethlehem. There was no famine in Bethlehem. The fields were full of waving grain, and busy servants were reaping it and gathering it up to bind into sheaves. Above all were the fields of the rich man, Boaz, shining with barley and corn.

Naomi and Ruth came to the edge of the fields and watched the busy reapers. They saw that after each sheaf was bound, and each pile of corn was stacked, a little grain fell to the ground. Ruth said to Naomi: "Let me go to the field and glean the ears of corn after them." And Naomi said to her, "Go, my daughter." And she went and came and gleaned in the field after the reapers.

And Boaz came from Bethlehem, and said to his reapers: "Whose damsel is this?" For he saw how very beautiful Ruth was, and how busily she was gleaning. The reapers said: "It is the damsel that came back with Naomi out of the land of the Moabites."

And Ruth ran up to Boaz, crying: "I pray you, let me glean and gather after the reapers among the sheaves."

And Boaz, who was good and kind, said to Ruth:

"Hearest thou not, my daughter? Go not to glean in any other field, but abide here."

Then Ruth bowed herself to the ground, and said: "Why have I found such favor in thine eyes, seeing I am a stranger?"

And Boaz answered her: "It hath been showed me all that thou hast done to thy mother."

So, all day, Ruth gleaned in Boaz's fields. At noon she ate bread and parched corn with the others. Boaz commanded his reapers to let fall large handfuls of grain, as they worked, for Ruth to gather, and at night she took it all home to Naomi.

"Where hast thou gleaned today?" asked Naomi when she saw the food that Ruth had brought to her.

"The man's name with whom I wrought today is Boaz," said Ruth. And Naomi said: "Blessed be he of the Lord—the man is near of kin unto us."

So Ruth gleaned daily, and at the end of the barley harvest the good man Boaz took Ruth and Naomi to live with him in his own house forever.

Written Summation

Model Practice 1

When Naomi saw that Ruth loved her so much, she forgot how tired and hungry she was.

So, all day, Ruth gleaned in Boaz's fields. At noon she ate bread and parched corn with the others.

Model Practice 2

Model Practice 3

A Story of Old Rome

c. 5th Century BC
from Fifty Famous People
by James Baldwin

There was a great famine in Rome. The summer had been very dry and the corn crop had failed. There was no bread in the city. The people were starving.

One day, to the great joy of all, some ships arrived from another country. These ships were loaded with corn. Here was food enough for all.

The rulers of the city met to decide what should be done with the corn. "Divide it among the poor people who need it so badly," said some. "Let it be a free gift to them from the city."

But one of the rulers was not willing to do this. His name was Coriolanus, and he was very rich.

"These people are poor because they have been too lazy to work," he said. "They do not deserve any gifts from the city. Let those who wish any corn bring money and buy it."

When the people heard about this speech of the rich man, Coriolanus, they were very angry.

"He is no true Roman," said some.

"He is selfish and unjust," said others.

"He is an enemy to the poor. Kill him! Kill him!" cried the mob. They did not kill him, but they drove him out of the city and bade him never return.

Coriolanus made his way to the city of Antium, which was not far from Rome. The people of Antium were enemies of the Romans and had often been at war with them. So they welcomed Coriolanus very kindly and made him the general of their army.

Coriolanus began at once to make ready for war against Rome. He persuaded other towns near Antium to send their soldiers to help him.

Soon, at the head of a very great army, he marched toward the city, which had once been his home. The rude soldiers of Antium overran all the country around Rome. They burned the villages and farmhouses. They filled the land with terror.

Coriolanus pitched his camp quite near to the city. His army was the greatest that the Romans had ever seen. They knew that they were helpless before so strong an enemy.

"Surrender your city to me," said Coriolanus. "Agree to obey the laws that I shall make for you. Do this, or I will burn Rome and destroy all its people."

The Romans answered, "We must have time to think of this matter. Give us a few days to learn what sort of laws you will make for us. And then we will say whether we can submit to them or not."

"I will give you thirty days to consider the matter," said Coriolanus.

Then he told them what laws he would require them to obey. These laws were so severe that all said, "It will be better to die at once."

At the end of the thirty days, four of the city's rulers went out to beg him to show mercy to the people of Rome. These rulers were old men, with wise faces and long white beards. They went out bareheaded and very humble.

Coriolanus would not listen to them. He drove them back with threats and told them that they should expect no mercy from him; but he agreed to give them three more days to consider the matter.

The next day, all the priests and learned men went out to beg for mercy. These were dressed in their long flowing robes, and all knelt humbly before him. But he drove them back with scornful words.

On the last day, the great army which Coriolanus had led from Antium was drawn up in battle array. It was ready to march upon the city and destroy it.

All Rome was in terror. There seemed to be no way to escape the anger of this furious man.

Then the rulers, in their despair, said, "Let us go up to the house where Coriolanus used to live when he was one of us. His mother and his wife are still there. They are noble women, and they love Rome. Let us ask them to go out and beg our enemy to have mercy upon us. His heart will be hard indeed if he can refuse his mother and his wife."

The two noble women were willing to do all that they could to save their city. So, leading his little children by the hand, they went out to meet Coriolanus. Behind them followed a long procession of the women of Rome. Coriolanus was in his tent. When he saw his mother and his wife and his children, he was filled with joy. But when they made known their errand, his face darkened, and he shook his head.

For a long time his mother pleaded with him. For a long time his wife begged him to be merciful. His little children clung to his knees and spoke loving words to him.

At last, he could hold out no longer. "O mother," he said, "you have saved your country, but have lost your son!" Then he commanded his army to march back to the city of Antium.

Rome was saved; but Coriolanus could never return to his home, his mother, his wife and children. He was lost to them.

Written Summation

Model Practice 1

Coriolanus was in his tent.
When he saw his mother
and his wife and his
children, he was filled
with joy.

For a long time his mother pleaded with him. For a long time his wife begged him to be merciful.

Model Practice 2

Model Practice 3

The Brave Three Hundred
c. 480 BC
from Fifty Famous Stories Retold
by James Baldwin

All Greece was in danger. A mighty army, led by the great King of Persia, had come from the east. It was marching along the seashore, and in a few days would be in Greece. The great king had sent messengers into every city and state, bidding them give him water and earth in token that the land and the sea were his. But they said,—

"No: we will be free."

And so there was a great stir throughout all the land. The men armed themselves and made haste to go out and drive back their foe; and the women staid at home, weeping and waiting, and trembling with fear.

There was only one way by which the Persian army could go into Greece on that side, and that was by a narrow pass between the mountains and the sea. This pass was guarded by Leonidas, the King of the Spartans, with three hundred Spartan soldiers.

Soon the Persian soldiers were seen coming. There were so many of them that no man could count them. How could a handful of men hope to stand against so great a host?

And yet Leonidas and his Spartans held their ground. They had made up their minds to die at their post. Some one brought them word that there were so many Persians that their arrows darkened the sun.

"So much the better," said the Spartans; "we shall fight in the shade."

Bravely they stood in the narrow pass. Bravely they faced their foes. To Spartans there was no such thing as fear. The Persians came forward, only to meet death at the points of their spears.

But one by one, the Spartans fell. At last, their spears were broken; yet still they stood side by side, fighting to the last. Some fought with swords, some with daggers, and some with only their fists and teeth.

All day long, the army of the Persians was kept at bay. But when the sun went down, there was not one Spartan left alive. Where they had stood there was only a heap of the slain, all bristled over with spears and arrows.

Twenty thousand Persian soldiers had fallen before that handful of men. And Greece was saved.

Thousands of years have passed since then; but men still like to tell the story of Leonidas and the brave three hundred who died for their country's sake.

Written Summation

Some one brought them word that there were so many Persians that their arrows darkened the sun.

Twenty thousand Persian soldiers had fallen before that handful of men. And Greece was saved.

Model Practice 2

Model Practice 3

Socrates and His House
c. 469 BC–399 BC
from Fifty Famous Stories Retold
by James Baldwin

There once lived in Greece a very wise man whose name was Socrates. Young men from all parts of the land went to him to learn wisdom from him; and he said so many pleasant things, and said them in so delightful a way, that no one ever grew tired of listening to him.

One summer he built himself a house, but it was so small that his neighbors wondered how he could be content with it.

"What is the reason," said they, "that you, who are so great a man, should build such a little box as this for your dwelling house?"

"Indeed, there may be little reason," said he; "but, small as the place is, I shall think myself happy if I can fill even it with true friends."

Written Summation

Model Practice 1

One summer he built

himself a house, but it was

so small that his neighbors

wondered how he could be

content with it.

"What is the reason," said they, "that you, who are so great a man, should build such a little box as this for your dwelling house?".

Model Practice 2

Model Practice 3

Two Great Painters

c. born 464 BC
from Fifty Famous People
by James Baldwin

There was once a painter whose name was Zeuxis. He could paint pictures so life-like that they were mistaken for the real things which they represented.

At one time, he painted the picture of some fruit which was so real that the birds flew down and pecked at it. This made him very proud of his skill.

"I am the only man in the world who can paint a picture so true to life," he said.

There was another famous artist whose name was Parrhasius. When he heard of the boast which Zeuxis had made, he said to himself, "I will see what I can do."

So he painted a beautiful picture which seemed to be covered with a curtain. Then he invited Zeuxis to come and see it.

Zeuxis looked at it closely. "Draw the curtain aside and show us the picture," he said.

Parrhasius laughed and answered, "The curtain is the picture."

"Well," said Zeuxis, "you have beaten me this time, and I shall boast no more. I deceived only the birds, but you have deceived me, a painter."

Some time after this, Zeuxis painted another wonderful picture. It was that of a boy carrying a basket of ripe red cherries. When he hung this painting outside of his door, some birds flew down and tried to carry the cherries away.

"Ah! This picture is a failure," he said. "For if the boy had been as well painted as the cherries, the birds would have been afraid to come near him."

Written Summation

Zeuxis looked at it closely. "Draw the curtain aside and show us the picture," he said.

When he hung this painting outside of his door, some birds flew down and tried to carry the cherries away.

Model Practice 2

Model Practice 3

The Story of Cincinnatus
457 BC
from Fifty Famous Stories Retold
by James Baldwin

There was a man named Cincinnatus who lived on a little farm not far from the city of Rome. He had once been rich and had held the highest office in the land; but in one way or another he had lost all his wealth. He was now so poor that he had to do all the work on his farm with his own hands. But in those days, it was thought to be a noble thing to till the soil.

Cincinnatus was so wise and just that everybody trusted him and asked his advice. And when any one was in trouble and did not know what to do, his neighbors would say,—

"Go and tell Cincinnatus. He will help you."

Now there lived among the mountains, not far away, a tribe of fierce, half-wild men, who were at war with the Roman people. They persuaded another tribe of bold warriors to help them, and then marched toward the city, plundering and robbing as they came. They boasted that they would tear down the walls of Rome, and burn the houses, and kill all the men, and make slaves of the women and children.

At first the Romans, who were very proud and brave, did not think there was much danger. Every man in Rome was a soldier, and the army which went out to fight the robbers was the finest in the world. No one staid at home with the women and children and boys but the white-haired "Fathers," as they were called, who made the laws for the city, and a small company of men who guarded the walls. Everybody thought that it would be an easy thing to drive the men of the mountains back to the place where they belonged.

But one morning five horsemen came riding down the road from the mountains. They rode with great speed; and both men and horses were covered with dust and blood. The watchman at the gate knew them and shouted to them as they galloped in. Why did they ride thus? And what had happened to the Roman army?

They did not answer him, but rode into the city and along the quiet streets; and everybody ran after them, eager to find out what was the matter. Rome was not a large city at that time; and soon they reached the market place where the white-haired Fathers were sitting. Then they leaped from their horses and told their story.

"Only yesterday," they said, "our army was marching through a narrow valley between two steep mountains. All at once a thousand savage men sprang out from among the rocks before us and above us. They had blocked up the way; and the pass was so narrow that we could not fight. We tried to come back; but they had blocked up the way on this side of us too. The fierce men of the mountains were before us and behind us, and they were throwing rocks down upon us from above. We had been caught in a trap. Then ten of us set spurs to our horses; and five of us forced our way through, but the other five fell before the spears of the mountain men. And now, O Roman Fathers! send help to our army at once, or every man will be slain, and our city will be taken."

"What shall we do?" said the white-haired Fathers. "Whom can we send but the guards and the boys? And who is wise enough to lead them, and thus save Rome?"

All shook their heads and were very grave; for it seemed as if there was no hope. Then one said, "Send for Cincinnatus. He will help us."

Cincinnatus was in the field plowing when the men who had been sent to him came in great haste. He stopped and greeted them kindly and waited for them to speak.

"Put on your cloak, Cincinnatus," they said, "and hear the words of the Roman people."

Then Cincinnatus wondered what they could mean. "Is all well with Rome?" he asked, and he called to his wife to bring him his cloak.

She brought the cloak, and Cincinnatus wiped the dust from his hands and arms and threw it over his shoulders. Then the men told their errand.

They told him how the army with all the noblest men of Rome had been entrapped in the mountain pass. They told him about the great danger the city was in. Then they said, "The people of Rome make you their ruler and the ruler of their city, to do with everything as you choose. And the Fathers bid you come at once and go out against our enemies, the fierce men of the mountains."

So Cincinnatus left his plow standing where it was and hurried to the city. When he passed through the streets and gave orders as to what should be done, some of the people were afraid, for they knew that he had all power in Rome to do what he pleased. But he armed the guards and the boys and went out at their head to fight the fierce mountain men and free the Roman army from the trap into which it had fallen.

A few days afterward there was great joy in Rome. There was good news from Cincinnatus. The men of the mountains had been beaten with great loss. They had been driven back into their own place.

And now the Roman army, with the boys and the guards, was coming home with banners flying and shouts of victory; and at their head rode Cincinnatus. He had saved Rome.

Cincinnatus might then have made himself king. For his word was law, and no man dared lift a finger against him. But, before the people could thank him enough for what he had done, he gave back the power to the white-haired Roman Fathers and went again to his little farm and his plow.

He had been the ruler of Rome for sixteen days.

Written Summation

Model Practice 1 (Adapted from the original)

All at once, a thousand

savage men sprang out

from among the rocks

before us and above us.

Cincinnatus might then have made himself king. For his word was law, and no man dared lift a finger against him..

Model Practice 2

Model Practice 3

Damon and Pythias
c. 432 BC – c. 367 BC
from Fifty Famous Stories Retold
by James Baldwin

A young man whose name was Pythias had done something which the tyrant Dionysius did not like. For this offense he was dragged to prison, and a day was set when he should be put to death. His home was far away, and he wanted very much to see his father and mother and friends before he died.

"Only give me leave to go home and say good-by to those whom I love," he said. "And then I will come back and give up my life."

The tyrant laughed at him.

"How can I know that you will keep your promise?" he said. "You only want to cheat me, and save yourself."

Then a young man whose name was Damon spoke and said,—

"O king! Put me in prison in place of my friend Pythias. And let him go to his own country to put his affairs in order and to bid his friends farewell. I know that he will come back as he promised, for he is a man who has never broken his word. But if he is not here on the day which you have set, then I will die in his stead."

The tyrant was surprised that anybody should make such an offer. He at last agreed to let Pythias go and gave orders that the young man Damon should be shut up in prison.

Time passed, and by and by the day drew near which had been set for Pythias to die; and he had not come back. The tyrant ordered the jailer to keep close watch upon Damon and not let him escape. But Damon did not try to escape. He still had faith in the truth and honor of his friend. He said, "If Pythias does not come back in time, it will not be his fault. It will be because he is hindered against his will."

At last the day came, and then the very hour. Damon was ready to die. His trust in his friend was as firm as ever; and he said that he did not grieve at having to suffer for one whom he loved so much.

Then the jailer came to lead him to his death; but at the same moment Pythias stood in the door. He had been delayed by storms and shipwreck, and he had feared that he was too late. He greeted Damon kindly and then gave himself into the hands of the jailer. He was happy because he thought that he had come in time, even though it was at the last moment.

The tyrant was not so bad but that he could see good in others. He felt that men who loved and trusted each other, as did Damon and Pythias, ought not to suffer unjustly. And so he set them both free.

"I would give all my wealth to have one such friend," he said.

Written Summation

Model Practice 1

He greeted Damon kindly

And then gave himself into

the hands of the jailer.

He felt that men who loved and trusted each other, as did Damon and Pythias, ought not to suffer unjustly. And so he set them both free.

Model Practice 2

Model Practice 3

The Sword of Damocles

c. 4th century BC
from Fifty Famous Stories Retold
by James Baldwin

There was once a king whose name was Dionysius. He was so unjust and cruel that he won for himself the name of tyrant. He knew that almost everybody hated him, and so he was always in dread lest some one should take his life.

But he was very rich, and he lived in a fine palace where there were many beautiful and costly things. And he was waited upon by a host of servants who were always ready to do his bidding. One day a friend of his, whose name was Damocles, said to him,—

"How happy you must be! You have here everything that any man could wish."

"Perhaps you would like to change places with me," said the tyrant.

"No, not that, O king!" said Damocles; "but I think, that, if I could only have your riches and your pleasures for one day, I should not want any greater happiness."

"Very well," said the tyrant. "You shall have them."

And so, the next day, Damocles was led into the palace, and all the servants were bidden to treat him as their master. He sat down at a table in the banquet hall, and rich foods were placed before him. Nothing was wanting that could give him pleasure. There were costly wines, beautiful flowers, rare perfumes, and delightful music. He rested himself among soft cushions and felt that he was the happiest man in all the world.

Then he chanced to raise his eyes toward the ceiling. What was it that was dangling above him, with its point almost touching his head? It was a sharp sword, and it was hung by only a single horsehair. What if the hair should break? There was danger every moment that it would do so.

The smile faded from the lips of Damocles. His face became ashy pale. His hands trembled. He wanted no more food; he could drink no more wine; he took no more delight in the music. He longed to be out of the palace, and away; he cared not where.

"What is the matter?" said the tyrant.

"That sword! That sword!" cried Damocles. He was so badly frightened that he dared not move.

"Yes," said Dionysius, "I know there is a sword above your head, and that it may fall at any moment. But why should that trouble you? I have a sword over my head all the time. I am every moment in dread lest something may cause me to lose my life."

"Let me go," said Damocles. "I now see that I was mistaken, and that the rich and powerful are not so happy as they seem. Let me go back to my old home in the poor little cottage among the mountains."

And so long as he lived, he never again wanted to be rich, or to change places, even for a moment, with the king.

Written Summation

Model Practice 1

The smile faded from the lips of Damocles. His face became ashy pale. His hands trembled.

"That sword! That sword!" cried Damocles. He was so badly frightened that he dared not move.

Model Practice 2

Model Practice 3

A Laconic Answer
382 BC – 336 BC
from Fifty Famous Stories Retold
by James Baldwin

Many miles beyond Rome there was a famous country which we call Greece. The people of Greece were not united like the Romans; but instead there were several states, each of which had its own rulers.

Some of the people in the southern part of the country were called Spartans, and they were noted for their simple habits and their bravery. The name of their land was Laconia, and so they were sometimes called Lacons.

One of the strange rules, which the Spartans had, was that they should speak briefly and never use more words than were needed. And so a short answer is often spoken of as being laconic; that is, as being such an answer as a Lacon would be likely to give.

There was in the northern part of Greece a land called Macedon; and this land was at one time ruled over by a war-like king named Philip.

Philip of Macedon wanted to become the master of all Greece. So he raised a great army, and made war upon the other states, until nearly all of them were forced to call him their king. Then he sent a letter to the Spartans in Laconia and said, "If I go down into your country, I will level your great city to the ground."

In a few days, an answer was brought back to him. When he opened the letter, he found only one word written there.

That word was "IF."

It was as much as to say, "We are not afraid of you so long as the little word 'if' stands in your way."

Written Summation

Model Practice 1

Some of the people in

the southern part of the

country were called

Spartans.

In a few days, an answer was brought back to him. When he opened the letter, he found only one word written there.

Model Practice 2

Model Practice 3

A Lesson in Justice

356 BC –323 BC
from Fifty Famous People
by James Baldwin

Alexander the king of Macedon wished to become the master of the whole world. He led his armies through many countries. He plundered cities, he burned towns, and he destroyed thousands of lives.

At last, far in the East, he came to a land of which he had never heard. The people there knew nothing about war and conquest. Although they were rich, they lived simply and were at peace with all the world.

The shah, or ruler of these people, went out to meet Alexander and welcome him to their country. He led the great king to his palace and begged that he would dine with him.

When they were seated at the table, the servants of the shah stood by to serve the meal. They brought in what seemed to be fruits, nuts, cakes, and other delicacies; but when Alexander would eat, he found that everything was made of gold.

"What!" said he. "Do you eat gold in this country?"

"We ourselves eat only common food," answered the shah. "But we have heard that it was the desire for gold which caused you to leave your own country; and so, we wish to satisfy your appetite."

"It was not for gold that I came here," said Alexander. "I came to learn the customs of your people."

"Very well, then," said the shah, "stay with me a little while and observe what you can."

While the shah and the king were talking, two countrymen came in. "My lord," said one, "we have had a disagreement and wish you to settle the matter."

"Tell me about it," said the shah.

"Well, it is this way," answered the man: "I bought a piece of ground from this neighbor of mine and paid him a fair price for it. Yesterday, when I was digging in it, I found a box full of gold and jewels. This treasure does not belong to me, for I bought only the ground; but when I offered it to my neighbor he refused it."

The second man then spoke up and said, "It is true that I sold him the ground, but I did not reserve anything he might find in it. The treasure is not mine, and therefore I am unwilling to take it."

The shah sat silent for a while, as if in thought. Then he said to the first man, "Have you a son?"

"Yes, a young man of promise," was the answer.

The shah turned to the second man: "Have you a daughter?"

"I have," answered the man, "--a beautiful girl."

"Well, then, this is my judgment. Let the son marry the daughter, if both agree, and give them the treasure as a wedding portion."

Alexander listened with great interest. "You have judged wisely and rightly," said he to the shah, "but in my own country we should have done differently."

"What would you have done?"

"Well, we should have thrown both men into prison, and the treasure would have been given to the king."

"And is that what you call justice?" asked the shah.

"We call it policy," said Alexander.

"Then let me ask you a question," said the shah. "Does the sun shine in your country?"

"Surely."

"Does the rain fall there?"

"Oh, yes!"

"Is it possible! But are there any gentle, harmless animals in your fields?"

"A great many."

"Then," said the shah, "it must be that the sun shines and the rain falls for the sake of these poor beasts; for men so unjust do not deserve such blessings."

Written Summation

Model Practice 1

"It was not for gold that I came here," said Alexander. "I came to learn the customs of your people."

"Well, then, this is my judgment. Let the son marry the daughter, if both agree, and give them the treasure as a wedding portion."

Model Practice 2

Model Practice 3

The Story of Regulus
died c. 250 BC
from Fifty Famous Stories Retold
by James Baldwin

On the other side of the sea from Rome there was once a great city named Carthage. The Roman people were never very friendly to the people of Carthage, and at last, a war began between them. For a long time it was hard to tell which would prove the stronger. First the Romans would gain a battle, and then the men of Carthage would gain a battle. And so the war went on for many years.

Among the Romans there was a brave general named Regulus. He was a man of whom it was said never broke his word. It so happened after a while, that Regulus was taken prisoner and carried to Carthage. Ill and very lonely, he dreamed of his wife and little children so far away beyond the sea; and he had but little hope of ever seeing them again. He loved his home dearly, but he believed that his first duty was to his country; and so he had left all, to fight in this cruel war.

He had lost a battle, it is true, and had been taken prisoner. Yet he knew that the Romans were gaining ground, and the people of Carthage were afraid of being beaten in the end. They had hired soldiers from other countries to help them. But even with these, they would not be able to fight much longer against Rome.

One day some of the rulers of Carthage came to the prison to talk with Regulus.

"We should like to make peace with the Roman people," they said. "We are sure that, if your rulers at home knew how the war is going, they would be glad to make peace with us. We will set you free and let you go home, if you will agree to do as we say."

"What is that?" asked Regulus.

"In the first place," they said, "you must tell the Romans about the battles which you have lost, and you must make it plain to them that they have not gained anything by the war. In the second place, you must promise us, that, if they will not make peace, you will come back to your prison."

"Very well," said Regulus. "I promise you that, if they will not make peace, I will come back to prison."

And so they let him go; for they knew that a great Roman would keep his word.

When he came to Rome, all the people greeted him gladly. His wife and children were very happy, for they thought that now they would not be parted again. The white-haired Fathers who made the laws for the city came to see him. They asked him about the war.

"I was sent from Carthage to ask you to make peace," he said. "But it will not be wise to make peace. True, we have been beaten in a few battles, but our army is gaining ground every day. The people of Carthage are afraid, and well they may be. Keep on with the war a little while longer, and Carthage shall be yours. As for me, I have come to bid my wife and children and Rome farewell. To-morrow I will start back to Carthage and to prison; for I have promised."

Then the Fathers tried to persuade him to stay.

"Let us send another man in your place," they said.

"Shall a Roman not keep his word?" answered Regulus. "I am ill, and at the best have not long to live. I will go back, as I promised."

His wife and little children wept, and his sons begged him not to leave them again.

"I have given my word," said Regulus. "The rest will be taken care of."

Then he bade them good-by and went bravely back to the prison and the cruel death, which he expected.

This was the kind of courage that made Rome the greatest city in the world.

Written Summation

Model Practice 1

"Let us send another man in your place," they said.

"Shall a Roman not keep his word?" answered Regulus.

His wife and little children wept, and his sons begged him not to leave them again.

Model Practice 2

Model Practice 3

Julius Caesar

100 BC - 44 BC
from <u>Fifty Famous Stories Retold</u>
by James Baldwin

Nearly two thousand years ago there lived in Rome a man whose name was Julius Caesar. He was the greatest of all the Romans.

Why was he so great?

He was a brave warrior, and had conquered many countries for Rome. He was wise in planning and in doing. He knew how to make men both love and fear him.

At last, he made himself the ruler of Rome. Some said that he wished to become its king. But the Romans at that time did not believe in kings.

Once when Caesar was passing through a little country village, all the men, women, and children of the place came out to see him. There were not more than fifty of them, all together, and they were led by their mayor, who told each one what to do.

These simple people stood by the roadside and watched Caesar pass. The mayor looked very proud and happy; for was he not the ruler of this village? He felt that he was almost as great a man as Cæsar himself.

They said, "See how that fellow struts at the head of his little flock!"

"Laugh as you will," said Cæsar, "he has reason to be proud. I would rather be the head man of a village than the second man in Rome!"

At another time, Caesar was crossing a narrow sea in a boat. Before he was halfway to the farther shore, a storm overtook him. The wind blew hard; the waves dashed high; the lightning flashed; the thunder rolled.

It seemed every minute as though the boat would sink. The captain was in great fright. He had crossed the sea many times, but never in such a storm as this. He trembled with fear; he could not guide the boat; he fell down upon his knees; he moaned, "All is lost! All is lost!"

But Caesar was not afraid. He bade the man get up and take his oars again.

"Why should you be afraid?" he said. "The boat will not be lost; for you have Caesar on board."

Written Summation

Model Practice 1

The wind blew hard;

the waves dashed high;

the lightning flashed; the

thunder rolled.

"Why should you be afraid?" he said. "The boat will not be lost; for you have Caesar on board."

Model Practice 2

Model Practice 3

The Visit of the Wise Men

c. 4 BC
from Matthew 2:1-12
adapted from Christmas in Legend and Story
by Elva S. Smith

Now when Jesus was born in Bethlehem of Judaea in the days of King Herod, there came wise men from the east to Jerusalem. They said, "Where is he that is born King of the Jews? For we have seen his star in the east. And we have come to worship him."

When King Herod heard these things, he was troubled, and all Jerusalem with him. So he had gathered all the chief priests and scribes of the people together. He demanded of them that they tell him where Christ should be born.

And they said to him, "In Bethlehem, for it is written by the prophet:

'And thou Bethlehem, in the land of Judah,
are not the least among the princes of Judah.
For out of thee shall come a Governor
who shall rule my people Israel.

Then Herod asked the wise men what time the star appeared. And he sent them to Bethlehem and said, "Go and search for the young child. And when ye have found him, bring me word again that I may come and worship him also."

When they had heard the king, they departed; and, lo, the star, which they saw in the east, went before them, till it came and stood over where the young child was.

When they saw the star, they rejoiced with exceeding great joy.

And when they were come into the house, they saw the young child with Mary his mother. And they fell down and worshipped him. And when they had opened their treasures, they offered unto him gifts: gold, frankincense, and myrrh.

When they departed, they returned to their own country another way. For they had been warned in a dream that they should not return to Herod.

Written Summation

Model Practice 1 (adapted from the original)

"Go and search for the young child. And when you have found him, bring me word again."

And when they were come into the house, they saw the young child with Mary his mother. And they fell down and worshipped him.

Model Practice 2

Model Practice 3

Androclus and the Lion
may be non-fictional 1st century CE
from Fifty Famous Stories Retold
by James Baldwin

In Rome, there was once a poor slave whose name was Androclus. His master was a cruel man, and so unkind to him that at last Androclus ran away.

He hid himself in a wild wood for many days; but there was no food to be found, and he grew so weak and sick that he thought he should die. So one day he crept into a cave and lay down, and soon he was fast asleep.

After a while, a great noise woke him up. A lion had come into the cave and was roaring loudly. Androclus was very much afraid, for he felt sure that the beast would kill him. Soon, however, he saw that the lion was not angry, but that he limped as though his foot hurt him.

Then Androclus grew so bold that he took hold of the lion's lame paw to see what was the matter. The lion stood quite still, and rubbed his head against the man's shoulder. He seemed to say,—

"I know that you will help me."

Androclus lifted the paw from the ground, and saw that in it was a long, sharp thorn, which hurt the lion so much. He took the end of the thorn in his fingers; then he gave a strong, quick pull and out it came. The lion was full of joy. He jumped about like a dog, and licked the hands and feet of his new friend.

Androclus was not at all afraid after this; and when night came, he and the lion lay down and slept side by side.

For a long time, the lion brought food to Androclus every day; and the two became such good friends, that Androclus found his new life a very happy one.

One day some soldiers who were passing through the wood found Androclus in the cave. They knew who he was, and so took him back to Rome.

It was the law at that time that every slave who ran away from his master should be made to fight a hungry lion. So a fierce lion was shut up for a while without food, and a time was set for the fight.

When the day came, thousands of people crowded to see the sport. They went to such places at that time very much as people now a days go to see a circus show or a game of baseball.

The door opened, and poor Androclus was brought in. He was almost dead with fear, for the roars of the lion could already be heard. He looked up, and saw that there was no pity in the thou-sands of faces around him.

Then the hungry lion rushed in. With a single bound, he reached the poor slave. Androclus gave a great cry, not of fear, but of gladness. It was his old friend, the lion of the cave.

The people, who had expected to see the man killed by the lion, were filled with wonder. They saw Androclus put his arms around the lion's neck; they saw the lion lie down at his feet, and lick them lovingly; they saw the great beast rub his head against the slave's face as though he wanted to be petted. They could not understand what it all meant.

After a while, they asked Androclus to tell them about it. So he stood up before them, and, with his arm around the lion's neck, told how he and the beast had lived together in the cave.

"I am a man," he said; "but no man has ever befriended me. This poor lion alone has been kind to me; and we love each other as brothers."

The people were not so bad that they could be cruel to the poor slave now. "Live and be free!" they cried. "Live and be free!"

Others cried, "Let the lion go free too! Give both of them their liberty!"

And so Androclus was set free, and the lion was given to him for his own. And they lived together in Rome for many years.

Written Summation

Model Practice 1

After a while, a great noise woke him up. A lion had come into the cave and was roaring loudly.

Androclus gave a great cry, not of fear, but of gladness. It was his old friend, the lion of the cave.

Model Practice 2

Model Practice 3

CHAPTER II

Aesop's Fables

The Bear and the Bees
by Aesop

A bear roaming the woods in search of berries happened on a fallen tree in which a swarm of bees had stored their honey. The bear began to nose around the log very carefully to find out if the bees were at home. Just then one of the swarm came home from the clover field with a load of sweets. Guessing what the bear was after, the bee flew at him, stung him sharply and then disappeared into the hollow log.

The bear lost his temper in an instant, and sprang upon the log tooth and claw, to destroy the nest. But this only brought out the whole swarm. The poor bear had to take to his heels, and he was able to save himself only by diving into a pool of water.

It is wiser to bear a single injury in silence than to provoke a thousand by flying into a rage.

Written Summation

Model Practice 1 (adapted from the original)

The bear began to nose

around the log very carefully

to find out if the bees were

at home.

It is wiser to bear a single injury in silence than to provoke a thousand by flying into a rage.

Model Practice 2

Model Practice 3

The Dog, the Cock, and the Fox

from The Aesop for Children
by Aesop

A dog and a cock, who were the best of friends, wished very much to see something of the world. So they decided to leave the farmyard and to set out into the world along the road that led to the woods. The two comrades traveled along in the very best of spirits and without meeting any adventure to speak of.

At nightfall the cock, looking for a place to roost, as was his custom, spied nearby a hollow tree that he thought would do very nicely for a night's lodging. The dog could creep inside and the cock would fly up on one of the branches. So said, so done, and both slept very comfortably.

With the first glimmer of dawn, the cock awoke. For the moment, he forgot just where he was. He thought he was still in the farmyard where it had been his duty to arouse the household at daybreak. So standing on tiptoes, he flapped his wings and crowed lustily. But instead of awakening the farmer, he awakened a fox not far off in the wood. The fox immediately had rosy visions of a very delicious breakfast. Hurrying to the tree where the cock was roosting, he said very politely:

"A hearty welcome to our woods, honored sir. I cannot tell you how glad I am to see you here. I am quite sure we shall become the closest of friends."

"I feel highly flattered, kind sir," replied the cock slyly. "If you will, please go around to the door of my house at the foot of the tree; my porter will let you in."

The hungry but unsuspecting fox went around the tree as he was told, and in a twinkling, the dog had seized him.

Those who try to deceive may expect to be paid in their own coin.

Written Summation

Model Practice 1

With the first glimmer of dawn, the cock awoke.

The fox immediately had rosy visions of a very delicious breakfast.

Model Practice 2

Model Practice 3

The Farmer and His Sons

from The Aesop for Children
by Aesop

A rich old farmer, who felt that he had not many more days to live, called his sons to his bedside.

"My sons," he said, "heed what I have to say to you. Do not on any account part with the estate that has belonged to our family for so many generations. Somewhere on it is hidden a rich treasure. I do not know the exact spot, but it is there, and you will surely find it. Spare no energy and leave no spot unturned in your search."

The father died, and no sooner was he in his grave than the sons set to work digging with all their might, turning up every foot of ground with their spades, and going over the whole farm two or three times.

No hidden gold did they find; but at harvest time when they had settled their accounts and had pocketed a rich profit far greater than that of any of their neighbors, they understood that the treasure their father had told them about was the wealth of a bountiful crop and that in their industry had they found the treasure.

Industry is itself a treasure.

Written Summation

Model Practice 1

Spare no energy and leave

no spot unturned in your

search.

No hidden gold did they find; but at harvest time, when they had settled their accounts, they pocketed a rich profit far greater than that of any of their neighbors.

Model Practice 2 (modified from the original)

Model Practice 3

The Lark and Her Young Ones
from The Aesop for Children
by Aesop

A lark made her nest in a field of young wheat. As the days passed, the wheat stalks grew tall and the young birds, too, grew in strength. Then one day, when the ripe golden grain waved in the breeze, the farmer and his son came into the field.

"This wheat is now ready for reaping," said the farmer. "We must call in our neighbors and friends to help us harvest it."

The young larks in their nest close by were much frightened, for they knew they would be in great danger if they did not leave the nest before the reapers came. When the mother lark returned with food for them, they told her what they had heard.

"Do not be frightened, children," said the mother lark. "If the farmer said he would call in his neighbors and friends to help him do his work, this wheat will not be reaped for a while yet."

A few days later, the wheat was so ripe that, when the wind shook the stalks, a hail of wheat grains came rustling down on the young larks' heads.

"If this wheat is not harvested at once," said the farmer, "we shall lose half the crop. We cannot wait any longer for help from our friends. Tomorrow we must set to work, ourselves."

When the young larks told their mother what they had heard that day, she said:

"Then we must be off at once. When a man decides to do his own work and not depend on any one else, then you may be sure there will be no more delay."

There was much fluttering and trying out of wings that afternoon, and at sunrise next day, when the farmer and his son cut down the grain, they found an empty nest.

Self-help is the best help.

Written Summation

Model Practice 1

As the days passed, the

wheat stalks grew tall and

the young birds, too, grew

in strength.

A few days later, the wheat was so ripe, that when the wind shook the stalks, a hail of wheat grains came rustling down on the young larks' heads.

Model Practice 2

Model Practice 3

Mercury and the Woodman
from The Aesop for Children
by Aesop

A poor woodman was cutting down a tree near the edge of a deep pool in the forest. It was late in the day and the woodman was tired. He had been working since sunrise, and his strokes were not so sure as they had been early that morning. Thus it happened that the axe slipped and flew out of his hands into the pool.

The woodman was in despair. The axe was all he possessed with which to make a living, and he had not money enough to buy a new one. As he stood wringing his hands and weeping, the god Mercury suddenly appeared and asked what the trouble was. The woodman told what had happened, and straightway the kind Mercury dived into the pool. When he came up again, he held a wonderful golden axe.

"Is this your axe?" Mercury asked the woodman.

"No," answered the honest woodman, "that is not my axe."

Mercury laid the golden axe on the bank and sprang back into the pool. This time he brought up an axe of silver, but the woodman declared again that his axe was just an ordinary one with a wooden handle.

Mercury dived down for the third time, and when he came up again he had the very axe that had been lost.

The poor woodman was very glad that his axe had been found and could not thank the kind god enough. Mercury was greatly pleased with the woodman's honesty.

"I admire your honesty," he said, "and as a reward you may have all three axes, the gold and the silver as well as your own."

The happy woodman returned to his home with his treasures, and soon the story of his good fortune was known to everybody in the village. Now there were several woodmen in the village who believed that they could easily win the same good fortune. They hurried out into the woods, one here, one there, and hiding their axes in the bushes, pretended they had lost them. Then they wept and wailed and called on Mercury to help them.

And indeed, Mercury did appear, first to this one, then to that. To each one he showed an axe of gold, and each one eagerly claimed it to be the one he had lost. But Mercury did not give them the golden axe. Oh no! Instead, he gave them each a hard whack over the head with it and sent them home. And when they returned the next day to look for their own axes, they were nowhere to be found.

Honesty is the best policy.

Written Summation

Model Practice 1

The woodman was in despair. The axe was all he possessed with which to make a living.

But Mercury did not give them the golden axe. Oh no! Instead, he gave them each a hard whack over the head with it and sent them home.

Model Practice 2

Model Practice 3

The Milkmaid and her Pail

from The Aesop for Children
by Aesop

A milkmaid had been out to milk the cows and was returning from the field with the shining milk pail balanced nicely on her head. As she walked along, her pretty head was busy with plans for the days to come.

"This good, rich milk," she mused, "will give me plenty of cream to churn. The butter I make I will take to market, and with the money I get for it, I will buy a lot of eggs for hatching. How nice it will be when they are all hatched and the yard is full of fine young chicks. Then when May Day comes, I will sell them, and with the money, I'll buy a lovely new dress to wear to the fair. All the young men will look at me. They will come and try to love me, but I shall very quickly send them about their business!"

As she thought of how she would settle that matter, she tossed her head scornfully, and down fell the pail of milk to the ground. And all the milk flowed out, and with it vanished butter and eggs and chicks and new dress and all the milkmaid's pride.

Do not count your chickens before they are hatched.

Written Summation

Model Practice 1 (adapted from the original)

Do not count your

chickens before they

are hatched.

As she walked along, her pretty head was busy with plans for the days to come.

Model Practice 2

Model Practice 3

The Miser

from <u>The Aesop for Children</u>
by Aesop

A miser had buried his gold in a secret place in his garden. Every day he went to the spot, dug up the treasure and counted it piece by piece to make sure it was all there. He made so many trips that a thief, who had been observing him, guessed what it was the miser had hidden, and one night quietly dug up the treasure and made off with it.

When the miser discovered his loss, he was overcome with grief and despair. He groaned and cried and tore his hair.

A passerby heard his cries and asked what had happened.

"My gold! O my gold!" cried the miser, wildly, "someone has robbed me!"

"Your gold! There in that hole? Why did you put it there? Why did you not keep it in the house where you could easily get it when you had to buy things?"

"Buy!" screamed the miser angrily. "Why, I never touched the gold. I couldn't think of spending any of it."

The stranger picked up a large stone and threw it into the hole.

"If that is the case," he said, "cover up that stone. It is worth just as much to you as the treasure you lost!"

A possession is worth no more than the use we make of it.

Written Summation

Model Practice 1 (adapted from the original)

When the miser

discovered his loss, he was

overcome with grief and

despair. He groaned and

cried and tore his hair.

"Buy!" screamed the miser angrily. "Why, I never touched the gold. I couldn't think of spending any of it."

Model Practice 2

Model Practice 3

The Monkey and the Dolphin
from The Aesop for Children
by Aesop

It happened once upon a time that a certain Greek ship bound for Athens was wrecked off the coast close to Piraeus, the port of Athens. Had it not been for the dolphins, who at that time were very friendly toward mankind and especially toward Athenians, all would have perished. But the dolphins took the shipwrecked people on their backs and swam with them to shore.

Now it was the custom among the Greeks to take their pet monkeys and dogs with them whenever they went on a voyage. So when one of the dolphins saw a monkey struggling in the water, he thought it was a man and made the monkey climb up on his back. Then off he swam with him toward the shore.

The monkey sat up, grave and dignified, on the dolphin's back.

"You are a citizen of illustrious Athens, are you not?" asked the dolphin politely.

"Yes," answered the monkey, proudly. "My family is one of the noblest in the city."

"Indeed," said the dolphin. "Then of course you often visit Piraeus."

"Yes, yes," replied the monkey. "Indeed, I do. I am with him constantly. Piraeus is my very best friend."

This answer took the dolphin by surprise, and, turning his head, he now saw what it was he was carrying. Without more ado, he dove and left the foolish monkey to take care of himself, while he swam off in search of some human being to save.

One falsehood leads to another.

Written Summation

Model Practice 1

The monkey sat up,

grave and dignified, on the

dolphin's back.

Without more ado, he dove and left the foolish monkey to take care of himself, while he swam off in search of some human being to save.

Model Practice 2

Model Practice 3

The North Wind and the Sun
from The Aesop for Children
by Aesop

The North Wind and the sun had a quarrel about which of them was the stronger. While they were disputing with much heat and bluster, a traveler passed along the road wrapped in a cloak.

"Let us agree," said the sun, "that he is the stronger who can strip that traveler of his cloak."

"Very well," growled the North Wind, and at once sent a cold, howling blast against the traveler.

With the first gust of wind, the ends of the cloak whipped about the traveler's body. But he immediately wrapped it closely around him, and the harder the wind blew, the tighter he held it to him. The North Wind tore angrily at the cloak, but all his efforts were in vain.

Then the sun began to shine. At first, his beams were gentle, and in the pleasant warmth after the bitter cold of the North Wind, the traveler unfastened his cloak and let it hang loosely from his shoulders. The sun's rays grew warmer and warmer. The man took off his cap and mopped his brow. At last, he became so heated that he pulled off his cloak, and, to escape the blazing sunshine, threw himself down in the welcome shade of a tree by the roadside.

Gentleness and kind persuasion win where force and bluster fail.

Written Summation

Model Practice 1 (adapted from the original sentence)

With the first gust of wind, the ends of the cloak whipped about the traveler's body.

But he immediately wrapped it closely around him, and the harder the wind blew, the tighter he held it to him.

Model Practice 2

Model Practice 3

The Shepherd Boy and the Wolf
from The Aesop for Children
by Aesop

A shepherd boy tended his master's sheep near a dark forest not far from the village. Soon he found life in the pasture very dull. All he could do to amuse himself was to talk to his dog or play on his shepherd's pipe.

One day as he sat watching the sheep and the quiet forest, and thinking what he would do should he see a wolf, he thought of a plan to amuse himself.

His master had told him to call for help should a wolf attack the flock, and the villagers would drive it away. So now, though he had not seen anything that even looked like a wolf, he ran toward the village shouting at the top of his voice, "Wolf! Wolf!"

As he expected, the villagers who heard the cry dropped their work and ran in great excitement to the pasture. But when they got there, they found the boy doubled up with laughter at the trick he had played on them.

A few days later, the shepherd boy again shouted, "Wolf! Wolf!" Again the villagers ran to help him, only to be laughed at again.

Then one evening as the sun was setting behind the forest and the shadows were creeping out over the pasture, a wolf really did spring from the underbrush and fall upon the sheep.

In terror, the boy ran toward the village shouting "Wolf! Wolf!" But though the villagers heard the cry, they did not run to help him as they had before. "He cannot fool us again," they said.

The wolf killed a great many of the boy's sheep and then slipped away into the forest.

Liars are not believed even when they speak the truth.

Written Summation

Model Practice 1

All he could do to amuse

himself was to talk to his

dog or play on his shepherd's

pipe.

A few days later, the shepherd boy again shouted, "Wolf! Wolf!" Again the villagers ran to help him, only to be laughed at again.

Model Practice 2

Model Practice 3

The Tortoise and the Ducks

from The Aesop for Children
by Aesop

The tortoise, you know, carries his house on his back. No matter how hard he tries, he cannot leave home. They say that Jupiter punished him so, because he was such a lazy stay-at-home that he would not go to Jupiter's wedding, even when especially invited.

After many years, tortoise began to wish he had gone to that wedding. When he saw how gaily the birds flew about and how the hare and the chipmunk and all the other animals ran nimbly by, always eager to see everything there was to be seen, the tortoise felt very sad and discontented. He wanted to see the world too, and there he was with a house on his back and little short legs that could hardly drag him along.

One day he met a pair of ducks and told them all his trouble.

"We can help you to see the world," said the ducks. "Take hold of this stick with your teeth and we will carry you far up in the air where you can see the whole countryside. But keep quiet or you will be sorry."

The tortoise was very glad indeed. He seized the stick firmly with his teeth, the two ducks took hold of it one at each end, and away they sailed up toward the clouds.

Just then a crow flew by. He was very much astonished at the strange sight and cried:

"This must surely be the King of Tortoises!"

"Why certainly——" began the tortoise.

But as he opened his mouth to say these foolish words he lost his hold on the stick, and down he fell to the ground, where he was dashed to pieces on a rock.

Foolish curiosity and vanity often lead to misfortune.

Written Summation

Model Practice 1

The tortoise, you know,

carries his house on his

back. No matter how hard

he tries, he cannot leave

home.

He wanted to see the world too, and there he was with a house on his back and short little legs that could hardly drag him along.

Model Practice 2

Model Practice 3

Two Travelers and a Bear
from The Aesop for Children
by Aesop

Two men were traveling in company through a forest, when, all at once, a huge bear crashed out of the brush near them.

One of the men, thinking of his own safety, climbed a tree.

The other, unable to fight the savage beast alone, threw himself on the ground and lay still, as if he were dead. He had heard that a bear would not touch a dead body.

It must have been true, for the bear sniffed at the man's head awhile, and then, seeming to be satisfied that he was dead, walked away.

The man in the tree climbed down.

"It looked just as if that bear whispered in your ear," he said. "What did he tell you?"

"He said," answered the other, "that it was not at all wise to keep company with a fellow who would desert his friend in a moment of danger."

Misfortune is the test of true friendship.

Written Summation

Model Practice 1

Two men were traveling in company through a forest, when, all at once, a huge bear crashed out of the brush near them.

It must have been true, for the bear sniffed at the man's head awhile, and then, seeming to be satisfied that he was dead, walked away.

Model Practice 2

Model Practice 3

The Vain Jackdaw and His Borrowed Feathers
from The Aesop for Children
by Aesop

A Jackdaw chanced to fly over the garden of the king's palace. There he saw with much wonder and envy a flock of royal peacocks in all the glory of their splendid plumage.

Now the black Jackdaw was not a very handsome bird, nor very refined in manner. Yet he imagined that all he needed to make himself fit for the society of the peacocks was a dress like theirs. So he picked up some castoff feathers of the peacocks and stuck them among his own black plumes.

Dressed in his borrowed finery he strutted loftily among the birds of his own kind. Then he flew down into the garden among the peacocks. But they soon saw who he was. Angry at the cheat, they flew at him, plucking away the borrowed feathers and also some of his own.

The poor Jackdaw returned sadly to his former companions. There another unpleasant surprise awaited him. They had not forgotten his superior airs toward them, and, to punish him, they drove him away with a rain of pecks and jeers.

Borrowed feathers do not make fine birds.

Written Summation

Model Practice 1 (adapted from the original)

Dressed in his borrowed finery, he strutted loftily among the birds of his own kind.

Angry at the cheat, they flew at him, plucking away the borrowed feathers and also some of his own.

Model Practice 2

Model Practice 3

Wolf and the Kid

from The Aesop for Children
by Aesop

There was once a little kid whose growing horns made him think he was a grown-up Billy Goat and able to take care of himself. So one evening when the flock started home from the pasture and his mother called, the kid paid no heed and kept right on nibbling the tender grass. A little later when he lifted his head, the flock was gone.

He was all alone. The sun was sinking. Long shadows came creeping over the ground. A chilly little wind came creeping with them making scary noises in the grass. The kid shivered as he thought of the terrible wolf. Then he started wildly over the field, bleating for his mother. But not halfway, near a clump of trees, there was the wolf!

The kid knew there was little hope for him.

"Please, Mr. Wolf," he said trembling, "I know you are going to eat me. But first please pipe me a tune, for I want to dance and be merry as long as I can."

The wolf liked the idea of a little music before eating; so he struck up a merry tune, and the kid leaped and frisked gaily.

Meanwhile, the flock was moving slowly homeward. In the still evening air, the wolf's piping carried far. The Shepherd Dogs pricked up their ears. They recognized the song the wolf sings before a feast, and in a moment, they were racing back to the pasture. The wolf's song ended suddenly, and as he ran, with the dogs at his heels, he called himself a fool for turning piper to please a kid, when he should have stuck to his butcher's trade.

Do not let anything turn you from your purpose.

Written Summation

Model Practice 1

He was all alone. The sun was sinking. Long shadows came creeping over the ground.

A chilly little wind came creeping with them making scary noises in the grass.

Model Practice 2

Model Practice 3

The Wolf and the Lean Dog

from The Aesop for Children
by Aesop

A wolf prowling near a village one evening met a dog. It happened to be a very lean and bony dog, and Master Wolf would have turned up his nose at such meager fare had he not been more hungry than usual. So he began to edge toward the dog, while the dog backed away.

"Let me remind your lordship," said the dog, his words interrupted now and then as he dodged a snap of the wolf's teeth, "how unpleasant it would be to eat me now. Look at my ribs. I am nothing but skin and bone. But let me tell you something in private. In a few days, my master will give a wedding feast for his only daughter. You can guess how fine and fat I will grow on the scraps from the table. Then is the time to eat me."

The wolf could not help thinking how nice it would be to have a fine fat dog to eat instead of the scrawny object before him. So he went away pulling in his belt and promising to return.

Some days later, the wolf came back for the promised feast. He found the dog in his master's yard, and asked him to come out and be eaten.

"Sir," said the dog, with a grin, "I shall be delighted to have you eat me. I'll be out as soon as the porter opens the door."

But the "porter" was a huge dog whom the wolf knew by painful experience to be very unkind toward wolves. So he decided not to wait and made off as fast as his legs could carry him.

Do not depend on the promises of those whose interest it is to deceive you.

Take what you can get when you can get it.

Written Summation

Model Practice 1 (adapted from the original sentence)

You can guess how fine and fat I will grow on the scraps from the table. Then is the time to eat me.

Some days later, the wolf came back for the promised feast. He found the dog in his master's yard, and asked him to come out and be eaten.

Model Practice 2

Model Practice 3

CHAPTER III

Poetry from or about Ancient History

Note: Poetry models should be written in the same manner that the author wrote them, meaning indentions and punctuation.

Each line of poetry should begin on a new line. If the student cannot fit the line of the model on one line, he should continue the sentence on the next line with an indention at the beginning.

For an example, see the model to "Age" on page III-4.

Age

by Anacreon
c. 570 BC – 480 BC
from the Library Of The World's Best Literature, Ancient And Modern, Vol. 2
by Charles Dudley Warner
Cowley's Translation.

>   Oft am I by the women told,
>   Poor Anacreon, thou grow'st old!
>   Look how thy hairs are falling all;
>   Poor Anacreon, how they fall!
>   Whether I grow old or no,
>   By th' effects I do not know;
>   This I know, without being told,
>   'Tis time to live, if I grow old;
>   'Tis time short pleasures now to take,
>   Of little life the best to make,
>   And manage wisely the last stake.

Of the life of this lyric poet we have little exact knowledge. We know that he was an Ionian Greek, and therefore by racial type a luxury-loving, music-loving Greek, born in the city of Teos on the coast of Asia Minor. The year was probably B.C. 562.

Anacreon was a lyrist of the first order. Plato's poet says of him in the 'Symposium,' "When I hear the verses of Sappho or Anacreon, I set down my cup for very shame of my own performance."

His metres, like his matter, are simple and easy. So imitators, perhaps as brilliant as the master, have sprung up and produced a mass of songs; and at this time it remains in doubt whether any complete poem of Anacreon remains untouched. For this reason the collection is commonly termed 'Anacreontics'.

Model Practice 1

This I know, without being

told,

'Tis time to live, if I

grow old.

'Tis time short pleasures now to take,
Of little life the best to make,
And manage wisely the last stake.

Model Practice 2

Model Practice 3

The Boaster

620 BC - 560 BC
by Aesop, W. J. Linton, and Walter Crane
from the Baby's Own Aesop 1887

In the house, in the market, the streets,
Everywhere he was boasting his feats;
Till one said, with a sneer,
"Let us see it done here!
What's so oft done with ease, one repeats."

Deeds not words.

Model Practice 1

In the house, in the market,

the streets,

Everywhere he was boasting

his feats;

Till one said, with a sneer,
"Let us see it done here!
What's so oft done with ease, one
repeats."

Model Practice 2

Model Practice 3

The Crow and the Pitcher
620 BC - 560 BC
by Aesop, W. J. Linton, and Walter Crane
from the Baby's Own Aesop 1887

How the cunning old crow got his drink
When 'twas low in the pitcher, just think!
Don't say that he spilled it!
With pebbles he filled it,
Till the water rose up to the brink.

Use your wits.

Model Practice 1

How the cunning old crow

got his drink

When 'twas low in the

pitcher, just think!

Don't say that he spilled it!
With pebbles he filled it,
Till the water rose up to the brink.

Model Practice 2

Model Practice 3

The Destruction of Sennacherib
reign 705-681 BC
by Lord Byron
from Children's Literature
edited by Charles Madison Curry and Erle Elsworth Clippinger
based on 2 Kings 18-19

The Assyrian came down like a wolf on the fold,
And his cohorts were gleaming in purple and gold;
And the sheen of their spears was like stars on the sea,
When the blue wave rolls nightly on deep Galilee.

Like the leaves of the forest when summer is green,
That host with their banners at sunset were seen:
Like the leaves of the forest when autumn hath blown,
The host on the morrow lay wither'd and strown.

For the Angel of Death spread his wings on the blast,
And breathed in the face of the foe as he passed;
And the eyes of the sleepers waxed deadly and chill,
And their hearts but once heaved, and for ever grew still!

And there lay the steed with his nostril all wide,
But through it there rolled not the breath of his pride:
And the foam of his gasping lay white on the turf,
And cold as the spray of the rock-beating surf.

And there lay the rider distorted and pale,
With the dew on his brow and the rust on his mail;
And the tents were all silent, the banners alone,
The lances unlifted, the trumpet unblown.

And the widows of Ashur are loud in their wail,
And the idols are broke in the temple of Baal;
And the might of the Gentile, unsmote by the sword,
Hath melted like snow in the glance of the Lord.

Model Practice 1

The Assyrian came down like

a wolf on the fold,

And his cohorts were

gleaming in purple and

gold;

And the sheen of their spears was like stars on the sea,
When the blue wave rolls nightly on deep Galilee.

Model Practice 2

Model Practice 3

Horatius (excerpt)
c. 6th Century BC
from Lays of Ancient Rome
by Thomas Babbington Macaulay

    A Lay Made About the Year Of The City CCCLX

        XXIX
"Haul down the bridge, Sir Consul,
    With all the speed ye may;
I, with two more to help me,
    Will hold the foe in play.
In yon strait path a thousand
    May well be stopped by three.
Now who will stand on either hand,
    And keep the bridge with me?"

        XXX
Then out spake Spurius Lartius;
    A Ramnian proud was he:
"Lo, I will stand at thy right hand,
    And keep the bridge with thee."
And out spake strong Herminius;
    Of Titian blood was he:
"I will abide on thy left side,
    And keep the bridge with thee."

        XXXI
"Horatius," quoth the Consul,
    "As thou sayest, so let it be."
And straight against that great array
    Forth went the dauntless Three.
For Romans in Rome's quarrel
    Spared neither land nor gold,
Nor son nor wife, nor limb nor life,
    In the brave days of old.

        LV
But with a crash like thunder
    Fell every loosened beam,
And, like a dam, the mighty wreck
    Lay right athwart the stream:
And a long shout of triumph
    Rose from the walls of Rome,
As to the highest turret-tops
    Was splashed the yellow foam.

LVI

And, like a horse unbroken
    When first he feels the rein,
The furious river struggled hard,
    And tossed his tawny mane,
And burst the curb and bounded,
    Rejoicing to be free,
And whirling down, in fierce career,
Battlement, and plank, and pier,
    Rushed headlong to the sea.

LVII

Alone stood brave Horatius,
    But constant still in mind;
Thrice thirty thousand foes before,
    And the broad flood behind.
"Down with him!" cried false Sextus,
    With a smile on his pale face.
"Now yield thee," cried Lars Porsena,
    "Now yield thee to our grace."

LVIX

"Oh, Tiber! Father Tiber!
    To whom the Romans pray,
A Roman's life, a Roman's arms,
    Take thou in charge this day!"
So he spake, and speaking sheathed
    The good sword by his side,
And with his harness on his back,
    Plunged headlong in the tide.

LX

No sound of joy or sorrow
    Was heard from either bank;
But friends and foes in dumb surprise,
With parted lips and straining eyes,
    Stood gazing where he sank;
And when above the surges,
    They saw his crest appear,
All Rome sent forth a rapturous cry,
And even the ranks of Tuscany
    Could scarce forbear to cheer.

Model Practice 1

And with his harness on

his back,

Plunged headlong in

the tide.

No sound of joy or sorrow
Was heard from either bank;

Model Practice 2

Model Practice 3

Moderation

65 BC-8 BC
translation of Horace, Bk. II. Ode X_. W. COWPER.
from the World's Best Poetry, Vol. 10
edited by Bliss Carman

He that holds fast the golden mean,
  And lives contentedly between
    The little and the great,
  Feels not the wants that pinch the poor,
  Nor plagues that haunt the rich man's door.

Model Practice 1 (adapted from the original)

He that holds fast the

golden mean,

And lives contentedly

between

Feels not the wants that pinch the poor,
Nor plagues that haunt the rich man's door.

Model Practice 2

Model Practice 3

The Mouse and the Lion
by Aesop, W. J. Linton, and Walter Crane
from the Baby's Own Aesop 1887

A poor thing the Mouse was, and yet,
When the Lion got caught in a net,
All his strength was no use
'Twas the poor little Mouse
Who nibbled him out of the net.

Small causes may produce great results.

Model Practice 1

A poor thing the Mouse

was, and yet,

When the Lion got caught

in a net,

All his strength was no use

'Twas the poor little Mouse
Who nibbled him out of the net.

Model Practice 2

Model Practice 3

The People Who Are Really Happy
from the Children's Bible
translated and arranged by Henry A. Sherman
Matthew 5:3-10
written c. 70 AD

Jesus said to his disciples:

"Blessed are the poor in spirit,
For theirs is the Kingdom of Heaven.
Blessed are the meek,
For they shall inherit the earth.
Blessed are they who mourn,
For they shall be comforted.
Blessed are they who hunger and thirst for righteousness,
For they shall be satisfied.
Blessed are the merciful,
For they shall receive mercy.
Blessed are the pure in heart,
For they shall see God.
Blessed are the peacemakers,
For they shall be called the sons of God.
Blessed are they who are persecuted because of their righteousness,
For theirs is the Kingdom of Heaven.
Blessed are you when you are reviled, persecuted, and falsely maligned because of loyalty to me;
Rejoice and be glad, for great is your reward in heaven, for so the prophets were persecuted who came before you."

Model Practice 1

Blessed are the poor in

spirit,

For theirs is the Kingdom

of Heaven.

Blessed are the meek,
For they shall inherit the earth.
Blessed are they who mourn,
For they shall be comforted.

Model Practice 2

Model Practice 3

Psalms 23 and 121

by King David
c.1037 - 967 BCE
from the King James Bible

Psalms 23

01 The LORD is my shepherd; I shall not want.
02 He maketh me to lie down in green pastures: he leadeth me beside the still waters.
03 He restoreth my soul: he leadeth me in the paths of righteousness for his name's sake.
04 Yea, though I walk through the valley of the shadow of death, I will fear no evil: for thou art with me; thy rod and thy staff they comfort me.
05 Thou preparest a table before me in the presence of mine enemies: thou anointest my head with oil; my cup runneth over.
06 Surely goodness and mercy shall follow me all the days of my life: and I will dwell in the house of the LORD for ever.

Psalms 121

01 I will lift up mine eyes unto the hills, from whence cometh my help.
02 My help cometh from the LORD, which made heaven and earth.
03 He will not suffer thy foot to be moved: he that keepeth thee will not slumber.
04 Behold, he that keepeth Israel shall neither slumber nor sleep.
05 The LORD is thy keeper: the LORD is thy shade upon thy right hand.
06 The sun shall not smite thee by day, nor the moon by night.
07 The LORD shall preserve thee from all evil: he shall preserve thy soul.
08 The LORD shall preserve thy going out and thy coming in from this time forth and even for evermore.

Model Practice 1

The Lord shall preserve

thee from all evil: he shall

preserve thy soul.

The Lord shall preserve thy going out and thy coming in from this time forth and even for evermore.

Model Practice 2

Model Practice 3

The Two Paths
from Proverbs IV
by Solomon
c. 1000 BCE - 931 BCE
from an Ontario Reader

Hear, O my son, and receive my sayings;
And the years of thy life shall be many.
I have taught thee in the way of wisdom;
I have led thee in paths of uprightness.
When thou goest, thy steps shall not be straitened;
And if thou runnest, thou shalt not stumble.
       Take fast hold of instruction;
       Let her not go:
       Keep her;
       For she is thy life.
Enter not into the Path of the Wicked,
And walk not in the way of evil men.
       Avoid it,
       Pass not by it;
       Turn from it,
       And pass on.
For they sleep not, except they have done mischief;
And their sleep is taken away, unless they cause some to fall.
For they eat the bread of wickedness,
And drink the wine of violence.
But the Path of the Righteous is as the light of dawn,
That shineth more and more unto the perfect day.
The way of the wicked is as darkness:
They know not at what they stumble.

Model Practice 1

Take fast hold of

instruction;

Let her not go:

Keep her;

For she is thy life.

Enter not into the Path of the
    Wicked,
And walk not in the way of evil men.

Model Practice 2

Model Practice 3

The Vision of Belshazzar
died 539 BC
from Journeys Through Bookland, Vol. 6
by Lord Byron

The King was on his throne,
    The Satraps(153-1) throng'd the hall;
A thousand bright lamps shone
    O'er that high festival.
A thousand cups of gold,
    In Judah deem'd divine—
Jehovah's vessels hold(154-2)
    The godless Heathen's wine.

In that same hour and hall
    The fingers of a Hand
Came forth against the wall,
    And wrote as if on sand:
The fingers of a man;—
    A solitary hand
Along the letters ran,
    And traced them like a wand.

The monarch saw, and shook,
    And bade no more rejoice;
All bloodless wax'd his look,
    And tremulous his voice:—
"Let the men of lore appear,
    The wisest of the earth,
And expound the words of fear,
    Which mar our royal mirth."

Chaldea's(154-3) seers are good,
    But here they have no skill;
And the unknown letters stood
    Untold and awful still.
And Babel's(154-4) men of age
    Are wise and deep in lore;
But now they were not sage,
    They saw—but knew no more.

A Captive in the land,
    A stranger and a youth,
He heard the king's command,
    He saw that writing's truth;
The lamps around were bright,
    The prophecy in view;
He read it on that night,—
    The morrow proved it true!

"Belshazzar's grave is made,
    His kingdom pass'd away,
He, in the balance weigh'd,
    Is light and worthless clay;
The shroud, his robe of state;
    His canopy, the stone:
The Mede is at his gate!
    The Persian on his throne!"

153-1 The satraps were the governors of the provinces, who ruled under the king and were accountable to him.
154-2 These were the sacred "vessels that were taken out of the temple of the house of God which was at Jerusalem."
154-3 The terms Chaldea and Babylonia were used practically synonymously.
154-4 Babel is a shortened form of Babylon.

Note.—According to the account given in the fifth chapter of *Daniel*, Belshazzar was the last king of Babylon, and the son of the great king Nebuchadnezzar, who had destroyed Jerusalem and taken the Jewish people captive to Babylon. The dramatic incident with which the second stanza of Byron's poem deals is thus described:
"In the same hour came forth fingers of a man's hand, and wrote over against the candlestick upon the plaister of the wall of the king's palace; and the king saw the part of the hand that wrote."
After all the Babylonian wise men had tried in vain to read the writing, the "captive in the land," Daniel, was sent for, and he interpreted the mystery.
"And this is the writing that was written, MENE, MENE, TEKEL, UPHARSIN.
"This is the interpretation of the thing: MENE; God hath numbered thy kingdom, and finished it.
"TEKEL; Thou art weighed in the balances, and art found wanting.
"PERES; Thy kingdom is divided, and given to the Medes and Persians."
The fulfillment of the prophecy thus declared by Daniel is described thus briefly: "In that night was Belshazzar the king of the Chaldeans slain. And Darius the Median took the kingdom."

Model Practice 1

In that same hour and hall

The fingers of a Hand

Came forth against the

wall,

And wrote as if on sand.

The fingers of a man;—
　A solitary hand
Along the letters ran,
　And traced them like a wand.

Model Practice 2

Model Practice 3

CHAPTER IV

Tales from Various Cultures

The Bag of Winds

from a <u>Story Hour Reader</u>
by Ida Coe and Alice J. Christie
Greek myth

The great caves of an island, far away in the midst of the sea, were the home of the winds.

Eolus was ruler of the winds. He kept them imprisoned in the caves. Sometimes he allowed them to go free for a time, to have a frolic or take exercise.

Although the winds were often unruly and were fond of mischief, they always obeyed the voice of Eolus.

North Wind was the roughest of all. He would go from his cave on the wildest errands.

Sometimes he would pile the waves mountains high and would lash them into a tempest. He would tear the sails and break the masts of the vessels. He would uproot the forest trees and tear the roofs from the houses.

But at the command of Eolus, North Wind would cease his roaring and would go sullenly back to his cave.

"South Wind!" Eolus would call. "Send a gentle, playful breeze among the flowers. Bring gay sunshine and soft showers. Sing a song of spring.

"West Wind! Blow steadily against the sails of the ships and speed them on their journey.

"East Wind! Go forth in a jolly, merry mood. Whirl the leaves over the ground and scatter the seeds far and wide.

"North Wind! Cover the earth with a blanket of snow. Freeze the waters of the lakes and rivers."

Thus Eolus would command the winds, and they would do his bidding.

One day a ship stopped near the island of the winds, and anchored. The captain of the ship and the sailors went ashore.

Eolus treated the visitors very kindly.

When the sailors discovered that they had come to the home of the winds, they cried, "O Eolus! Tell West Wind to blow and help us reach home quickly:"

Then Eolus took a leather bag and put into it all the unruly winds. He tied the end of the bag with a silver string. Giving the bag to the captain, he said, "Fasten the bag to the mast of your ship. Do not open it, or trouble will follow."

Then Eolus called West Wind from his island cave.

The captain and the sailors thanked Eolus and started off in the ship. West Wind blew gently, and the ship sailed over smooth waters day and night. Each day found them nearer home.

At last, on the evening of the ninth day, they saw the shores of their own land.

The captain cried, "Land, ahoy! We shall anchor in the harbor tomorrow."

Tired with long watching, and thinking that the ship was safe, he went to sleep.

Then the sailors began to whisper softly to each other.

"What do you suppose there is in the bag?" said one.

"It is tied with a silver cord. I am sure that it is full of gold," said another.

Then they planned to rob the captain of his treasure.

One of the sailors untied the bag.

Out rushed the angry winds! They raged and roared. A storm arose, and the ship was sent far out of its course. The captain begged West Wind to help the sailors, but he could not.

At last the ship was driven back to the home of the winds.

Eolus was surprised when he saw the ship again.

"Why have you returned?" asked Eolus.

"The sailors untied the silver cord at the end of the bag and set the unruly winds free," replied the captain. "Please call them back to their caves and help us."

"Depart!" cried Eolus angrily. "I will show you no more favors."

Sadly they sailed away, and no kind West Wind helped them.

They toiled for many days and nights, and they suffered great hardship before they came once more in sight of their own land.

Written Summation

Model Practice 1

Out rushed the angry winds! They raged and roared. A storm arose, and the ship was sent far out of its course.

"Depart!" cried Eolus angrily. "I will show you no more favors."

Model Practice 2

Model Practice 3

Diana and Apollo

adapted from a <u>Story Hour Reader</u>
by Ida Coe and Alice J. Christie
Roman myth

On an island in the sea, there lived a beautiful woman who had two children. They were twins—a boy and a girl. The girl's name was Diana, the boy's Apollo.

It was a floating island. Neptune, the king of the sea, had placed four marble pillars under it. Then he had fastened it with heavy chains.

The two children grew quickly. Diana became tall and lovely. Jupiter, king of heaven and earth, saw that she was very fair.

One day Diana was walking through the forest. Jupiter met her and spoke to her. He said, "Fair Diana, from now on you shall be called Queen of the Woods."

Diana, followed by her maids the wood nymphs, often roamed through the forest. She took care of the deer and all helpless creatures, but she hunted fierce animals.

Apollo, also, grew to be fair and strong.

Jupiter gave many gifts to the youth. He gave Apollo a pair of swans and a golden chariot. With them, the boy could go anywhere on land or sea.

The most wonderful present that Jupiter gave to Apollo was a silver bow with sharp arrows. The arrows never missed their mark. Apollo prized the bow highly and used it skillfully. Later he came to be called "Master of the Silver Bow."

Written Summation

Model Practice 1

Jupiter gave many gifts to the youth. He gave Apollo a pair of swans and a golden chariot.

The arrows never missed their mark. Apollo prized the bow highly and used it skillfully.

Model Practice 2

Model Practice 3

The Dog and the Dog Dealer
from Good Stories for Great Holidays by Frances Jenkins Olcott
by Ramaswami Raju
tale of India

A dog was standing by the cottage of a peasant. A man who dealt in dogs passed by the way. The dog said, "Will you buy me?"

The man said, "Oh, you ugly little thing! I would not give a quarter of a penny for you!"

Then the dog went to the palace of the king and stood by the portal. The sentinel caressed it, and said, "You are a charming little creature!"

Just then, the dog dealer came by. The dog said, "Will you buy me?"

"Oh," said the man, "you guard the palace of the king, who must have paid a high price for you. I cannot afford to pay the amount, else I would willingly take you."

"Ah!" said the dog, "how place and position affect people!"

Written Summation

Just then, the dog dealer came by. The dog said, "Will you buy me?"

"Ah!" said the dog, "how place and position affect people!"

Model Practice 2

Model Practice 3

The Golden Touch

from a <u>Beacon Reader</u>
by James H. Fassett
Greek Myth

Many years ago there lived a king named Midas.

King Midas had one little daughter, whose name was Marigold.

King Midas was very, very rich. It was said that he had more gold than any other king in the world. One room of his great castle was almost filled with yellow gold pieces.

At last the king grew so fond of his gold that he loved it better than anything else in all the world. He even loved it better than his own little daughter, dear little rosy-cheeked Marigold. His one great wish seemed to be for more and more gold.

One day while he was in his gold room counting his money, a beautiful fairy boy stood before him.

The boy's face shone with a wonderful light, and he had wings on his cap and wings on his feet. In his hand he carried a strange-looking wand, and the wand also had wings.

"Midas, you are the richest man in the world," said the fairy. "There is no king who has so much gold as you."

"That may be," said the king. "As you see, I have this room full of gold, but I should like much more; for gold is the best and the most wonderful thing in the world."

"Are you sure?" asked the fairy.

"I am very sure," answered the king.

"If I should grant you one wish," said the fairy, "would you ask for more gold?"

"If I could have but one wish," said the king, "I would ask that everything I touched should turn to beautiful yellow gold."

"Your wish shall be granted," said the fairy "At sunrise to-morrow morning your slightest touch will turn everything into gold. But I warn you that your gift will not make you happy."

"I will take the risk," said the king.

The next morning King Midas awoke very early. He was eager to see if the fairy's promise had come true.

As soon as the sun arose he tried the gift by touching the bed lightly with his hand. The bed turned to gold.

All was gold, gold, gold. He touched the chair and table. Upon the instant they were turned to solid gold. The king was wild with joy.

He ran around the room, touching everything he could see. His magic gift turned all to shining, yellow gold.

The king soon felt hungry and went down to eat his breakfast. Now a strange thing happened. When he raised a glass of clear cold water to drink, it became solid gold. Not a drop of water could pass his lips.

The bread turned to gold under his fingers. The meat was hard, and yellow, and shiny. Not a thing could he get to eat. All was gold, gold, gold.

His little daughter came running in from the garden. Of all living creatures she was the dearest to him.

He touched her hair with his lips. At once the little girl was changed to a golden statue.

A great fear crept into the king's heart, sweeping all the joy out of his life. In his grief he called and called upon the fairy who had given him the gift of the golden touch.

"O Fairy," he begged, "take away this horrible golden gift! Take all my lands. Take all my gold. Take everything, only give me back my little daughter."

In a moment the beautiful fairy was standing before him.

"Do you still think that gold is the greatest thing in the world?" asked the fairy.

"No! No!" cried the king. "I hate the very sight of the yellow stuff."

"Are you sure that you no longer wish the golden touch?" asked the fairy.

"I have learned my lesson," said the king. "I no longer think gold the greatest thing in the world."

"Very well," said the fairy, "take this pitcher to the spring in the garden and fill it with water. Then sprinkle those things which you have touched and turned to gold."

The king took the pitcher and rushed to the spring. Running back, he first sprinkled the head of his dear little girl. Instantly she became his own darling Marigold again, and gave him a kiss.

The king sprinkled the golden food, and to his great joy it turned back to real bread and real butter.

Then he and his little daughter sat down to breakfast. How good the cold water tasted. How eagerly the hungry king ate the bread and butter, the meat, and all the good food.

The king hated his golden touch so much that he sprinkled even the chairs and the tables and everything else that the fairy's gift had turned to gold.

Written Summation

Model Practice 1

"No! No!" cried the king. "I hate the very sight of the yellow stuff."

How eagerly the hungry king ate the bread and butter, the meat, and all the good food.

Model Practice 2

Model Practice 3

Great and Little Bear
adapted from a Story Hour Reader
by Ida Coe and Alice J. Christie
Greek myth

Callisto was a beautiful woman. And the god Jupiter admired her.

Soon the goddess Juno saw that Jupiter was kind to Callisto. She became very angry.

"I will take away her beauty, so that no one shall admire her," said Juno.

Night and day she thought and planned. Before long she found a way to punish Callisto.

One morning the fair and gentle Callisto was picking wild flowers in a field. Suddenly, she was changed into a bear. She was driven into a forest nearby.

"You shall live in this forest forever! A cave under the rocks shall be your home!" cried Juno.

Although she had the form of a bear, Callisto was still a woman at heart. She feared all the animals that she met.

The hunting dogs scared her, and she would hide in terror from the hunters.

One day a young man was hunting in the forest. Callisto saw at once that he was her son Arcas.

She rushed toward her son to hold him. But Arcas thought the bear was going to attack him, so he lifted his hunting spear.

As he was about to strike the bear, Jupiter appeared. The god snatched away the spear just in time to save Callisto's life.

Jupiter took both Callisto and Arcas and placed them in the sky. Callisto became the Great Bear, and Arcas the Little Bear.

They have remained in the sky ever since. On pleasant nights you can see them in the sky, as they move around the North Star.

Written Summation

Model Practice 1

Suddenly, she was changed

into a bear. She was driven

into a forest nearby.

"You shall live in this forest forever! A cave under the rocks shall be your home!" cried Juno.

Model Practice 2

Model Practice 3

Sennin the Hermit

from a Story Hour Reader
by Ida Coe and Alice J. Christie
tale of Japan

In the far-away land of Japan, there was a little village that lay at the foot of a high mountain.

Every day the children went to play on the grassy bank near a pond at one end of the village. They threw stones into the water. They fished, and they sailed their toy boats. They picked the wild flowers that grew in the fields nearby.

They carried with them rice to eat. And from morning until evening they played near the pond.

One day, while they were at play, the children were surprised to see an old man with a long, white beard walking toward them. He came from the direction of the mountain.

The children stopped their games to watch the old man. He came into their midst, and patting them upon their heads, easily made them his friends.

The children continued their play, for they knew that the old man was kind.

The man watched the children, and when it was time for them to go home, he said, "Come to the flat rock on the side of the mountain tomorrow, and I will show you some wonderful games."

Then he climbed up the mountain once more and disappeared.

The following morning, the children went to the flat rock. They found the old man waiting for them.

"Now, my dear children," said he, "I am going to amuse you. Look here!"

He picked up some dry sticks. He blew at the ends of the sticks, and at once they became sprays of beautiful cherry, plum, and peach blossoms. He passed a branch of each of the flowers to the girls.

Then he took a stone and threw it into the air. The stone turned into a dove!

Another stone became an eagle, another a nightingale, or any bird a boy chose to name.

"Now," said the old man, "I will show you some animals that I am sure will make you laugh."

The children clapped their hands.

He recited some verses, and a company of monkeys came leaping upon the rock. The monkeys jumped about, grinning at the same time and performing funny tricks.

The children clapped their hands again.

Then the old man bowed to them and said, "Children, I can play no more games today. It is time for you to go back to the village. Farewell!"

The old man turned to go. He went up the mountain in the direction of a cave. The children tried to follow him, but in spite of his age he was more nimble than they. They ran far enough, however, to see him enter the cave.

When they reached the entrance, the old man had disappeared.

The cave was surrounded by fragrant flowers; but into its depths the children did not dare to go.

Suddenly one of the girls pointed upwards, crying, "There is the old grandfather!"

The others looked up, and there, standing on a cloud over the top of the mountain, was the old man.

"Let us go home now," said one of the boys.

On the way, they met two men of the village, whom their parents had sent to search for them.

When the children had told their story, one of the men exclaimed, "Ah, happy children! The kind old man is surely Sennin, the wonderful Hermit of the Mountain!"

Written Summation

Model Practice 1

Then he took a stone
and threw it into the air.
The stone turned into a
dove!

The monkeys jumped about, grinning at the same time and performing funny tricks.

Model Practice 2

Model Practice 3

The Tricky Wolf and the Rats

from More Jataka Tales
retold by Ellen C. Babbitt

Once upon a time a big rat lived in the forest. And many hundreds of other rats called him their Chief.

A tricky wolf saw this troop of rats and began to plan how he could catch them. He wanted to eat them, but how was he to get them? At last he thought of a plan. He went to a corner near the home of the rats and waited until he saw one of them coming. Then he stood up on his hind legs.

The Chief of the Rats said to the wolf, "Wolf, why do you stand on your hind legs?"

"Because I am lame," said the tricky wolf. "It hurts me to stand on my front legs."

"And why do you keep your mouth open?" asked the rat.

"I keep my mouth open so that I may drink in all the air I can," said the wolf. "I live on air; it is my only food day after day. I cannot run or walk, so I stay here. I try not to complain." When the rats went away the Wolf lay down.

The Chief of the Rats was sorry for the wolf. And he went each night and morning with all the other rats to talk with the wolf, who seemed so poor, and who did not complain.

Each time as the rats were leaving, the wolf caught and ate the last one. Then he wiped his lips, and looked as if nothing had happened.

Each night there were fewer rats at bedtime. Then they asked the Chief of the Rats what the trouble was. He could not be sure, but he thought the wolf was to blame.

So the next day the Chief said to the other rats, "You go first this time and I will go last."

They did so, and as the Chief of the Rats went by, the wolf made a spring at him. But the wolf was not quick enough, and the Chief of the Rats got away.

"So this is the food you eat. Your legs are not so lame as they were. You have played your last trick, wolf," said the Chief of the Rats, springing at the wolf's throat. He bit the wolf, so that he died. And ever after the rats lived happily in peace and quiet.

Written Summation

Model Practice 1

But the wolf was not quick enough, and the Chief of the Rats got away.

"So this is the food you eat. Your legs are not so lame as they were. You have played your last trick, wolf," said the Chief of the Rats.

Model Practice 2

Model Practice 3

APPENDIX

Models Only

For Teacher Use

Oral Narration Questions
(Your student may not need these questions, if he can retell the story easily.)

Questions for Chapter I, historical narratives, or Chapter IV, cultural tales.

1. Who was the main character? (Who is the story about?)
2. What was the character like? (What was he or she like?)
3. Where was the character? (Where did the story happen?)
4. What time was it in the story? Time of day? Time of year?
5. Who else was in the story?
6. Does the main character have an enemy? What is the enemy's name? (Is there a bad guy?) (The enemy may also be self or nature.)
7. Does the main character want something? If not, does the main character have a problem?
8. What does the main character do? What does he say? If there are others, what do they do or say?
9. Why does the character do what he does?
10. What happens to the character as he tries to solve his problem?
11. Does the main character solve his problem? How does he solve his problem?
12. What happens at the end of the story?
13. Is there a moral to the story? If so, what was it?

Questions for Chapter III, poetry.
1. Is the poem about a character, an event, or an idea? (Is the poem about a person, place, or thing?)
2. Does this poem express a feeling of happiness, sadness, anger, excitement, joy, hope, determination, or fear?
3. How does the poem make you feel?
4. Do you think the author of the poem had a message?
5. What do you think the message of the poem is?

Written Summations
(Have your student sum up the story in no more than six sentences—two for each question.)

1. What happened at the beginning of the story?
2. What happened at the middle of the story?
3. What happened at the end of the story?

Principle of Praise
Encourage, build up, praise, and celebrate your student's successes.

Let no corrupt communication
proceed out of your mouth, but
that which is good to the use of edifying,
that it may minister grace
unto the hearers

Using the Grammar Guide

On the following page I have included a guide to introducing the eight parts of speech and basic punctuation. Complete grammar study with copywork. For some students, especially first graders, teaching only the first few months of material will be enough. **Feel free to focus on the material covered in month one for two months or longer.** Have your student:

1. Read the model.
2. Copy the model.
3. Return to the model and circle the correct parts of speech in the proper colors. See page 4.
4. **For older students only,** have them label the parts of speech according to the definitions below.

Label   Definition

nouns   **DO, IO, PN**   **direct object, indirect object, or predicate nominative**

Subject is the noun that is or does something. (Who ran? What stinks?)	I ran. **The dog** stinks.
Direct objects answers what. (I ate what?)	I ate **the cookie**.
Indirect objects tell for whom the action of the verb was done.	I gave **her** the cookie.
Predicate Nominative (Noun LinkingVerb Noun.)	John is my **dad**.

verbs   **AV, SB, LV**   **action verb, state of being, or linking verb**

Action verbs with a direct object are transitive verbs.	(He kicked the ball.)
Action verbs without a direct object are intransitive.	(He kicked.)
State of being verbs are the "to be" verbs.	(am, are, is, was, were, be, being, been)
Helping verbs help the main verb express time and mood.	(do run, can clean, am eating, might hit)
Linking verbs link the subject to the predicate.	(The wind grew chilly. The wind was chilly.)
	(If I can replace grew with was, it is a LV.)

pronouns   **SP, OP, PP, DP**   **Subject, Object, Possessive, Demonstrative**

Subject Pronouns	I, you, he, she, it, we, they	We love to read. It was outside.
Object Pronouns	me, you, him, her, it, us, them	She took it. I handed them the candy.
Possessive Pronouns	mine, yours, his, hers, theirs, ours, its, whose	That is **mine**! Ours is blue.
Demonstrative Pronouns	this, that, these, those	**That** is mine! We love that.

adjectives   **AA, PA, DA**   **Attributive, Predicate, or Demonstrative Adjectives**

Attributive Adjectives modify the noun and are right next to it.	(The **big** car.)
Predicate Adjectives follow linking verbs.	(The car is **big**.)
Demonstrative Adjectives (This, that, these, those)	**That** flower grew.

adverbs   **where, how, when, extent**

Adverbs that tell where, how, and when modify an adverb.	(up, down, quickly, softly, yesterday, now)
Adverbs that tell extent modify an adverb or adjective.	(almost, also, only, very, enough, rather, too)

prepositions **OP**   **object of the preposition**

GRAMMAR GUIDE
Optional: At the start of each month place memory work on flashcards

Month 1 — Nouns

All
- Memorize the definition of a noun below.
- Give your student examples of a noun.
- Have him give you examples.
- Work with your student to identify the nouns in the copywork model.
- Circle the nouns blue.
- Teach your student about capitalization.

Older students
- Teach the difference between a common noun and a proper noun.

Nouns <u>circle blue</u> — a word that names a person, place, thing, or idea

- Common nouns: (man), city, car, happiness
- Proper nouns: David, Lake Charles, Mustang

Capitalization — Beginning of a sentence, I, proper nouns.

Month 2 — Verbs

All
- Review the definition of a noun.
- Memorize the definition of a verb below.
- Give your student examples of verbs.
- Have him give you examples.
- Work with your student to identify the verbs in the copywork model.
- Circle the nouns blue and the verbs red.

Younger students
- You may choose to teach only action verbs.

Older students
- Teach the different types of verbs: action, state of being, linking, and helping verbs.
- Memorize state of being verbs
- Memorize list of helping verbs

Verbs <u>circle red</u> — a word that expresses action, state of being, or links two words together

- Action verbs: (jump), run, think, have, skip, throw, say, dance, smell
- State of being: any form of to be = **am, are, is, was, were, be, being, been**
- Linking verbs: **any state of being verb** and any verb that can logically be replaced by a "to be" verb. She **seems** nice. She is nice. The flower **smells** stinky. The flower is stinky.
- Helping verbs: am, are, is, was, were, be, being, been, do, does, did, has, have, had, may, might, must shall, will, can, should, would, could

Month 3   *Pronouns*

All	Review the definitions of nouns and verbs.
	Memorize the definition of a pronoun below.
	Give your student examples of pronouns.
	Have him give you examples.
	Help your student to identify the pronouns in the copywork model.
	Circle the nouns blue, the verbs red, and the pronouns green.
All	Teach the four types of sentences.

Pronouns <u>circle green</u>   a word that replaces a noun in a sentence. It may take the place of a person, place, thing, or idea.

Jack ran.	**He** ran.
Ike hit Al and Mary.	Ike hit **them**
The car is very nice.	**That** is very nice.

Types of sentences and punctuation

Declarative or statement	I have a blue dress. The ground is wet from the rain.
Interrogative or question	Will we have dessert today? What time is it?
Imperative or demand	Come here. Sit down. Mop the floor at 2:00.
Exclamation	I sold my painting for ten million dollars!

Month 4   *Adjectives*

All	Review the definitions of a noun, verb, and pronouns.
	Memorize the definition of an adjective below.
	Give your student examples of adjectives.
	Have him give you examples.
	Help your student to identify the adjectives in the copywork model.
	Circle the nouns blue, the verbs red, pronouns green, and the adjectives yellow.
All	Review the four types of sentences.
Older students	Learn about Attributive, Predicate, or Demonstrative Adjectives

Adjectives <u>circle yellow</u>   a word that describes a noun or a pronoun

(When studying adverbs, you may have your student draw an arrow to the word being modified.)

I want candy.	I want **five** candies.	
the car	the **red** car	Attributive adj. (adjective is before the noun)
I like shoes.	I like **those** shoes.	Demonstrative adj. (this, that, these, those)
The tall girl	The girl is **tall**.	Predicate adjectives (tall, stinky, angry)
The stinky dog	The dog smells **stinky**.	
The angry man	The man appeared **angry**.	

Month 5 — Adverbs

All
Review the definitions of nouns, verbs, pronouns, adjectives
Memorize the definition of an adverb below.
Give your student examples of adverbs.
Have him give you examples.
Help your student to identify the adverbs in the copywork model.
Circle the nouns blue, the verbs red, pronouns green, adjectives yellow, and adverbs orange.

Older students
Learn about possessive pronouns and possessive nouns

Adverbs <u>circle orange</u> a word that describes a verb, another adverb, or an adjective

Don't run.	Don't run **inside**.	**Modifies the verb** — tells where
The man ran.	The man ran **swiftly**.	tells how
It will rain.	It will rain **soon**.	tells when
The dog is hairy.	The dog is **very** hairy.	**Modifies adjectives or other adverbs** — tells extent (modifies hairy)

Possessives words that show ownership

Mine, yours, his, hers, ours, theirs, whose	possessive pronouns (used alone)
My car, **your** house, **his** shirt, **her** computer	possessive pronouns (used with a noun)
Jane's car, Mike's shoes, Jesus' parables,	singular possessive nouns
Mom and Dad's sons, my sisters' names, children's books	plural possessive nouns

Month 6 — Prepositions

All
Review the definitions of nouns, verbs, pronouns, adjectives, adverbs
Memorize the definition of a preposition below.
Give your student examples of prepositions.
Have him give you examples.
Help your student to identify the prepositions in the copywork model.
Circle the nouns blue, the verbs red, pronouns green, adjectives yellow, adverbs orange, and prepositions purple.

Older students
Learn about prepositional phrases and commas
Underline the prepositional phrase in the model.
Memorize list of prepositions

Preposition <u>circle purple</u> a word that shows relationship between one noun and another word in the sentence (Prepositional phrases are to be underlined)

He is <u>**on** the box</u>.   He is <u>**under** the box</u>.   He went <u>**around** the box</u>.   He is <u>**in** the box</u>.

Commas   3 items or more in a series
The elephant**,** the mouse**,** and the gnat are best friends.
I like red**,** green**,** and orange vegetables.

Common Prepositions
About, above, across, after, against along, among, around, at, before, behind, below, beneath, beside, between, beyond, by, down, during, except, for, from, in, inside, into, like, near, of, off, on, onto, out, over, past, since, through, throughout, to, toward, under, underneath, until, up, upon, with, within, without

Month 7 — Conjunctions

All	Review the definitions of nouns, verbs, pronouns, adjectives, adverbs, and prepositions
	Memorize the definition of a conjunction below.
	Give your student examples of conjunctions.
	Have him give you examples.
	Help your student to identify the conjunctions in the copywork model.
	Circle the nouns blue, the verbs red, pronouns green, adjectives yellow, adverbs orange, prepositions purple, and the conjunctions brown.
Older students	Learn Quotations marks

Conjunction <u>circle brown</u>   a word that links words, phrases, or clauses **(and, but, or, nor, so, for, yet)**

Jamie **and** I left. **(words)**
The blue sky, the warm sun, **and** the rainbow of flowers brightened my spirits. **(phrases)**
He is tall, **for** both of his parents are tall.
   (independent clauses, must have a comma when combining main clauses)

Quotation Marks   Use quotation marks to set off direct quotations.

"No, I don't like peas," answered the little boy.   beginning of a sentence
The little boy answered, "I don't like peas."   end of a sentence
"No," answered the little boy, "I don't like peas."   middle of a sentence

Month 8 — Interjections

All	Review the definitions of nouns, verbs, pronouns, adjectives, adverbs, prepositions, and conjunctions
	Memorize the definition of an interjection below.
	Give your student examples of interjections.
	Have him give you examples.
	Help your student to identify the interjections in the copywork model.
	Circle the nouns blue, the verbs red, pronouns green, adjectives yellow, adverbs orange, prepositions purple, conjunctions brown, and interjections black.
Older students	Learn semi-colon use

Interjection <u>circle black</u>   a word that expresses emotion, sometimes but not always, sudden or intense.

Yes! I want ice cream too! **Well**, we're late because the car broke down.

Semi-colons   replace commas and conjunctions when combining two independent clauses

My family is going to the farm**,** **and** we are going to have a grand time riding horses.
My family is going to the farm**;** we are going to have a grand time riding horses.

Models from Chapter I

Note: (In Chapters I and IV, models taken from the beginning of a paragraph are indented as well as models from one line dialogue.)

from **The Goddess of the Silkworm**
from A Child's World Reader
by Hetty Browne, Sarah Withers, and W K. Tate

In those days, the Chinese people wore clothes made of skins. By and by, the animals grew scarce.

The next morning Hoangti and the empress walked under the trees again. They found some worms still winding thread.

from **The Mystery of the Lost Brother**
adapted from The Wonder Book of Bible Stories
by Logan Marshall

When Joseph's brothers found that they were taken into Joseph's house, they were filled with fear.

Then Joseph placed his arms around Benjamin's neck, kissed him and wept upon him. And Benjamin wept on his neck.

from **David and Goliath**
adapted from a Beacon Reader
adapted from The Bible by James H. Fassett

Although David was only a boy, he was tall and strong and brave. When he knew he was in the right, he feared nothing.

David looked across the valley to the camp of the Philistines. There he saw a huge soldier dressed in shining armor.

from **Saved by a Dolphin**
adapted from Fifty Famous People
by James Baldwin

The sea was rough. The ship was driven far out of her course. Many days passed before they came in sight of land.

But they had made up their minds to get rid of him. They feared to spare him lest he should report the matter to the king.

from **The General and the Fox**
from Fifty Famous People
by James Baldwin

On a mountain near their city, there was a narrow chasm or hole in the rocks. It was very deep.

The rocky walls surrounded him on every side. There was no place where he could set his foot to climb out.

from "BECOS! BECOS! BECOS!"
from Fifty Famous People
   by James Baldwin

It was in our country that the first men and women lived," they said. "All the people of the world were once Egyptians."

The shepherd did as he was bidden. He took the children far away to a green valley where his flocks were feeding.

from A Clever Slave
from Fifty Famous People
   by James Baldwin

He was a small man with a large head and long arms. His face was white, but very homely. His large eyes were bright and snappy.

Aesop at once chose the largest one. The other slaves laughed and said he was foolish.

from The Young Cupbearer
from Fifty Famous People
   by James Baldwin

King Astyages smiled. He saw that Cyrus had a will of his own, and this pleased him very much.

He knew how to work with his hands. He ate only the plainest food. And he slept on a hard bed.

from The Lover of Men
from Fifty Famous People
   by James Baldwin

He knew only of those things that give joy and health and peace.

They passed out into the open country and saw the cottages of the poor people.

from The Boy and the Robbers (adapted from the original)
from Fifty Famous People
   by James Baldwin

Suddenly, towards evening, a band of robbers swooped down upon them. The merchants were not fighting men. They could do nothing.

"If I had answered your questions differently, I should have told a lie," said Otanes; "and none but cowards tell lies."

from Horatius at the Bridge
from Fifty Famous Stories Retold
   by James Baldwin

A dart thrown by one of Porsena's soldiers put out his left eye, but he did not falter.

But he was a strong man and the best swimmer in Rome. The next minute he rose.

from **The Story of Ruth and Naomi**
adapted from Good Cheer Stories Every Child Should Know
adapted from The Bible by C. S. Bailey and C. M. Lewis

When Naomi saw that Ruth loved her so much, she forgot how tired and hungry she was.

So, all day, Ruth gleaned in Boaz's fields. At noon she ate bread and parched corn with the others.

from **A Story of Old Rome**
from Fifty Famous People
by James Baldwin

Coriolanus was in his tent. When he saw his mother and his wife and his children, he was filled with joy.

For a long time his mother pleaded with him. For a long time his wife begged him to be merciful.

from **The Brave Three Hundred**
from Fifty Famous Stories Retold
by James Baldwin

Some one brought them word that there were so many Persians that their arrows darkened the sun.

Twenty thousand Persian soldiers had fallen before that handful of men. And Greece was saved.

from **Socrates and His House**
from Fifty Famous Stories Retold
by James Baldwin

One summer he built himself a house, but it was so small that his neighbors wondered how he could be content with it.

"What is the reason," said they, "that you, who are so great a man, should build such a little box as this for your dwelling house?"

from **Two Great Painters**
from Fifty Famous People
by James Baldwin

Zeuxis looked at it closely. "Draw the curtain aside and show us the picture," he said.

When he hung this painting outside of his door, some birds flew down and tried to carry the cherries away.

from **The Story of Cincinnatus**
from <u>Fifty Famous Stories Retold</u>
  by James Baldwin

All at once, a thousand savage men sprang out from among the rocks before and above us.

Cincinnatus might then have made himself king. For his word was law, and no man dared lift a finger against him.

from **Damon and Pythias**
from <u>Fifty Famous Stories Retold</u>
  by James Baldwin

He greeted Damon kindly and then gave himself into the hands of the jailer.

He felt that men who loved and trusted each other, as did Damon and Pythias, ought not to suffer unjustly. And so he set them both free.

from **The Sword of Damocles**
from <u>Fifty Famous Stories Retold</u>
  by James Baldwin

The smile faded from the lips of Damocles. His face became ashy pale. His hands trembled.

"That sword! That sword! cried Damocles. He was so badly frightened that he dared not move.

from **A Laconic Answer**
from <u>Fifty Famous Stories Retold</u>
  by James Baldwin

Some of the people in the southern part of the country were called Spartans.

In a few days, an answer was brought back to him. When he opened the letter, he found only one word written there.

from **A Lesson in Justice**
from <u>Fifty Famous People</u>
  by James Baldwin

"It was not for gold that I came here," said Alexander. "I came to learn the customs of your people."

"Well, then, this is my judgment. Let the son marry the daughter, if both agree, and give them the treasure as a wedding portion."

from **The Story of Regulus**
from <u>Fifty Famous Stories Retold</u>
  by James Baldwin

"Let us send another man in your place," they said.
"Shall a Roman not keep his word?" answered Regulus.

His wife and little children wept, and his sons begged him not to leave them again.

from **Julius Caesar**
from Fifty Famous Stories Retold
   by James Baldwin

The wind blew hard; the waves dashed high; the lightning flashed; the thunder rolled.

"Why should you be afraid?" he said. "The boat will not be lost; for you have Caesar on board."

from **The Visit of the Wise Men** (adapted from the original)
from Matthew 2:1-12
adapted from Christmas in Legend and Story
   by Elva S. Smith

Go and search for the young child. And when ye have found him, bring me word again.

And when they were come into the house, they saw the young child with Mary his mother. And they fell down and worshipped him.

from **Androclus and the Lion**
from Fifty Famous Stories Retold
   by James Baldwin

After a while, a great noise woke him up. A lion had come into the cave and was roaring loudly.

Androclus gave a great cry, not of fear, but of gladness. It was his old friend, the lion of the cave.

Models from Chapter II
from The Aesop for Children
b Aesop and Milo Winter

from The Bear and the Bees
The bear began to nose around the log very carefully to find out if the bees were at home.

It is wiser to bear a single injury in silence than to provoke a thousand by flying into a rage.

from The Dog, the Cock, and the Fox
With the first glimmer of dawn, the cock awoke.

The fox immediately had rosy visions of a very delicious breakfast.

from The Farmer and His Sons
Spare no energy and leave no spot unturned in your search.

No hidden gold did they find; but at harvest time, when they had settled their accounts, they pocketed a rich profit far greater than that of any of their neighbors.

from The Lark and Her Young Ones
As the days passed, the wheat stalks grew tall and the young birds, too, grew in strength.

A few days later, the wheat was so ripe, that when the wind shook the stalks, a hail of wheat grains came rustling down on the young larks' heads.

from Mercury and the Woodman
by E. A. Wallis Budge
The woodman was in despair. The axe was all he possessed with which to make a living.

But Mercury did not give them the golden axe. Oh no! Instead, he gave them each a hard whack over the head with it and sent them home.

from The Milkmaid and Her Pail
Do not count your chickens before they are hatched.

As she walked along, her pretty head was busy with plans for the days to come.

from The Miser
When the mister discovered his loss, he was overcome with grief and despair. He groaned and cried and tore his hair.

"Buy!" screamed the miser angrily. "Why, I never touched the gold. I couldn't think of spending any of it."

from The Monkey and the Dolphin
The monkey sat up, grave and dignified, on the Dolphin's back.

Without more ado, he dove and left the foolish monkey to take care of himself, while he swam off in search of some human being to save.

from The North Wind and the Sun
With the first gust of wind, the ends of the cloak whipped about the traveler's body.

But he immediately wrapped it closely around him, and th eharder the wind blew, the tighter he held it to him.

from The Shepherd Boy and the Wolf
All he could do to amuse himself was to talk to his dog or play on his shepherd's pipe.

A few days later, the shepherd boy again shouted, "Wolf! Wolf!" Again the Villagers ran to help him, only to be laughed at again.

from The Tortoise and the Ducks
The tortoise, you know, carries his house on his back. No matter how hard he tries, he cannot leave home.

He wanted to see the world too, and there he was with a house on his back and short little legs that could hardly drag him along.

from Two Travelers and a Bear
Two men were traveling in company through a forest, when, all at once, a huge bear crashed out of the brush near them.

It must have been true, for the bear snuffed at the man's head awhile, and then, seeming to be satisfied that he was dead, walked away.

from The Vain Jackdaw and His Borrowed Feathers
Dressed in his borrowed finery, he strutted loftily among the birds of his own kind.

Angry at the cheat, they flew at him, plucking away the borrowed feathers and also some of his own.

from Wolf and the Kid
He was all alone. The sun was sinking. Long shadows came creeping over the ground.

A chilly little wind came creeping with them making scary noises in the grass

from Wolf and the Lean Dog
You can guess how fine and fat I will grow on the scraps from the table. Then is the time to eat me.

Some days later, the wolf came back for the promised feast. He found the dog in his master's yard, and asked him to come out and be eaten.

Models from Chapter III

from Age
by Anacreon
from The Library Of The World's Best Literature, Ancient And Modern, Vol. 2
by Charles Dudley Warner, Cowley's Translation.

This I know, without being told,
'Tis time to live, if I grow old;

'Tis time short pleasures now to take,
Of little life the best to make,
And manage wisely the last stake.

from The Boaster
by Aesop, W. J. Linton, and Walter Crane
from The Baby's Own Aesop 1887

In the house, in the market, the streets,
Everywhere he was boasting his feats;

Till one said, with a sneer,
"Let us see it done here!
What's so oft done with ease, one repeats."

from The Crow and the Pitcher
by Aesop, W. J. Linton, and Walter Crane
from The Baby's Own Aesop 1887

How the cunning old Crow got his drink
When 'twas low in the pitcher, just think!

Don't say that he spilled it!
With pebbles he filled it,
Till the water rose up to the brink.

from The Destruction of Sennacherib
by Lord Byron
from Children's Literature
edited by Charles Madison Curry and Erle Elsworth Clippinger

The Assyrian came down like a wolf on the fold,
And his cohorts were gleaming in purple and gold;

And the sheen of their spears was like stars on the sea,
When the blue wave rolls nightly on deep Galilee.

from **Horatius (excerpt)**
from Lays of Ancient Rome
by Thomas Babbington Macaulay

And with his harness on his back,
  Plunged headlong in the tide.

No sound of joy or sorrow
  Was heard from either bank;

adapted from **Moderation**
translation of Horace, Bk. II. Ode X_. W. COWPER.
from The World's Best Poetry, Vol. 10
edited by Bliss Carman

He that holds fast the golden mean,
  And lives contentedly between

Feels not the wants that pinch the poor,
Nor plagues that haunt the rich man's door.

from **The Mouse and the Lion**
by Aesop, W. J. Linton, and Walter Crane
from The Baby's Own Aesop 1887

A poor thing the Mouse was, and yet,
When the Lion got caught in a net,
All his strength was no use

'Twas the poor little Mouse
Who nibbled him out of the net.

from **The People Who Are Really Happy**
from The Children's Bible
translated by Henry A. Sherman

Blessed are the poor in spirit,
For theirs is the Kingdom of Heaven.

Blessed are the meek,
For they shall inherit the earth.
Blessed are they who mourn,
For they shall be comforted.

from **Psalms 23 and 121**
by King David
from The King James Bible

The Lord shall preserve thee from all evil: he shall preserve thy soul.

The Lord shall preserve thy going out and thy coming in from this time forth and even for evermore.

from **The Two Paths**
from Proverbs IV
by Solomon
from an Ontario Reader

Take fast hold of instruction;
Let her not go:
Keep her;
For she is thy life.

Enter not into the Path of the Wicked,
And walk not in the way of evil men.

from **The Vision of Belshazzar**
from Journeys Through Bookland, Vol. 6
by Lord Byron

In that same hour and hall
   The fingers of a Hand
Came forth against the wall,
   And wrote as if on sand:

The fingers of a man;—
   A solitary hand
Along the letters ran,
   And traced them like a wand.

Models from Chapter IV

from **The Bag of Winds**
from A Story Hour Reader
    by Ida Coe and Alice J. Christie

Out rushed the angry winds! They raged and roared. A storm arose, and the ship was sent far out of its course.

"Depart!" cried Eolus angrily. "I will show you no more favors."

from **Diana and Apollo**
adapted from A Story Hour Reader
    by Ida Coe and Alice J. Christie

Jupiter gave many gifts to the youth. He gave Apollo a pair of swans and a golden chariot.

The arrows never missed their mark. Apollo prized the bow highly and used it skillfully.

from **The Dog and the Dog Dealer**
from Good Stories for Great Holidays by Frances Jenkins Olcott
    by Ramaswami Raju

Just then, the dog dealer came by. The dog said, "Will you buy me?"

"Ah!" said the dog, "how place and position affect people!"

from **The Golden Touch**
from A Beacon Reader
    by James H. Fassett

"No! No!" cried the king. "I hate the very sight of the yellow stuff."

How eagerly the hungry king ate the bread and butter, the meat, and all the good food.

from **Great and Little Bear**
adapted from A Story Hour Reader
    by Ida Coe and Alice J. Christie

Suddenly, she was changed into a bear. She was driven into a forest nearby.

"You shall live in this forest forever! A cave under the rocks shall be your home!" cried Juno.

from **Sennin the Hermit**
   from <u>A Story Hour Reader</u>
     by Ida Coe and Alice J. Christie

Then he took a stone and threw it into the air. The stone turned into a dove!

The monkeys jumped about, grinning at the same time and performing funny tricks.

from **The Tricky Wolf and the Rats**
   from <u>More Jataka Tales</u>
    retold by Ellen C. Babbitt

But the wolf was not quick enough, and the Chief of the Rats got away.

   "So this is the food you eat. Your legs are not so lame as they were. You have played your last trick, wolf," said the Chief of the Rats.

www.ingramcontent.com/pod-product-compliance
Lightning Source LLC
Chambersburg PA
CBHW081839230426
43669CB00018B/2760